PERPETUAL HUNGER

"This is an excellent book on successful selling – practical, helpful and fast-acting. Read it. Practice it. Boost your income immediately."

Brian Tracy
Author, Ultimate Sales Success, San Diego, CA, USA

"In his new book, Perpetual Hunger, Patrick Tinney challenges and motivates us to give more to get more – focusing the salesperson on methods for identifying and obtaining new customers. Tinney explains through example the limitless value created through the formation of high trust relationships - and the impact it will have on your wallet.

Rather than risk commoditization, Tinney identifies the levers that sales leaders deploy to gain the advantage by obtaining the number one negotiating position. Perpetual Hunger is essential reading for sales professionals, entrepreneurs, and everyone committed to identifying, contacting, influencing, qualifying, and cultivating profitable new customer relationships.

Besides enlightening the reader on the process and benefits of effective prospecting, Perpetual Hunger reinforces the lessons in his first volume, Unlocking Yes. Yet another winner from the Sales Master, Patrick Tinney!"

Ed "Skip" McLaughlin
Entrepreneur, Fortune 100 Executive and Author, The Purpose Is Profit: The Truth About Starting and Building Your Own Business, Darien, CT, USA

"Patrick has developed a very comprehensive but easy to follow guide for sales professionals and entrepreneurs. This is a must read for anyone interested in understanding how to sell your message, independent of what level of experience you may already have."

Michael Skinner
President & CEO, Greater Peterborough Innovation Cluster, Peterborough, ON Canada

"Perpetual Hunger gives readers passionate and enlightened strategy on sales prospecting and will inspire a vast audience of readers including sales professionals, entrepreneurs and start-ups. The book provides an A-to-Z lesson approach and includes twelve lesson exercises that readers can use to master transforming their sales prospecting weaknesses into strengths. Step-by-step, Patrick Tinney's stay hungry plan of attack theme provides real life examples of his own sales prospecting pain points which lead readers to valuable insight on how he navigated turning weaknesses into money-making strategies.

Readers will discover the importance of dealing with rejection, building relationships and trust, listening, understanding price traps, planning, rehearsing and managing stress. The book helps you get inside your head as well as inside the head of your prospect. Then the magic happens!

Perpetual Hunger also provides much more including how to network in today's marketplace and the advantage of using social media platforms and content strategy to strengthen your personal brand. The storytelling theme also discovered throughout the book is very compelling and will hold your attention.

This is a great new addition to Patrick Tinney's earlier book "Unlocking Yes" and will be the most valuable reference guide that any sales professional will own. If you want to stay ahead of the pack pick up a copy now and go make money. Be Brave, Bold, Strong and Stay Hungry!"

Audrey DeSisto
Founder and CEO, Digital Marketing Stream, Burlington, MA, USA

The more I dug into Patrick Tinney's new book Perpetual Hunger: Sales Prospecting Lessons & Strategy, the more I got out of it. Tinney's book stands out from the countless books about how to sell because he draws in the reader with his personal accounts of what it really means to be hungry, out there prospecting for sales. Then, he gives you not only the strategies to use, but also the tools to implement the strategies in a myriad of selling situations.

Tinney deftly weaves together the art and science of selling, delving into the factual (IQ) and emotional intelligence (EQ) you need to become a successful salesperson. Each lesson gives you clearly defined instructions and then asks you questions so that you can prepare yourself to go out and sell.

Of particular interest to me was Tinney's recommendation to do a SWOT analysis of your prospect before meeting with him or her. Armed with the results of the SWOT, you can truly understand your prospect's perspective. Tinney explains that only by understanding the people you are selling to and their needs and fears can you make the sale.

I recommend Perpetual Hunger to anyone who needs to understand how to meet customers, build trust, and convince them to buy from you.

Wyn Lydecker
Owner, Upstart Business Planning and Co-Author of
The Purpose Is Profit: The Truth About Starting and Building Your Own Business,
Darien, CT, USA

"Patrick's second book Perpetual Hunger: Sales Prospecting Lessons & Strategy provides excellent training and motivation for anyone in sales. Sales prospecting is the first step in the sales process, before account management, consultative sales or complex negotiations take place. Yet they all dovetail and Patrick demonstrates how smart prospecting lays the groundwork for building solid sales results and client relationships. The book provides bite-sized lessons and exercises the reader can work through. I recommend this book to people who are starting in sales and those who are well into their sales careers. There is a wealth of detail in "Perpetual Hunger"."

Steve Macfarlane
Vice President, Junction Digital Inc. Toronto, ON, Canada

"Every professional whose success depends on sales revenue will be inspired by Patrick's vast experience in prospecting, presenting and closing deals. Perpetual Hunger is the perfect pick-me-up regardless of your experience and position. My copy is now full of yellow highlights from cover to cover for future reference and important reminders. Bottom line... Read it and WIN."

Randy Craig
Founder, Decassia Consultants Inc., Toronto, ON, Canada

PERPETUAL HUNGER

Sales Prospecting

Lessons & Strategy

PERPETUAL HUNGER

Sales Prospecting

Lessons & Strategy

Patrick Tinney

2016

First Printing: 2016

ISBN 978-0-9938284-3-0

Centroid Publishing

STN Main, 150 King Street P.O. Box 713
Peterborough, Ontario, Canada K9J 6Z8
www.centroidmarketing.com

Ordering Information:

Special discounts are available on quantity purchases by corporations, associations, educators, and others. For details, contact the publisher at the above listed address.

U.S. trade bookstores and wholesalers: Please contact
Centroid Publishing
Tel: 1-705-657-2518
E-mail: patrick@centroidmarketing.com

DEDICATION

The world of business fascinates and challenges us in ways we never imagine. An interesting fact about the Internet is the enormous groups of silent followers who read our work and interact with us through social media. The Hon. Tamer Hegazy, Minister, Global Entrepreneurship was a silent observer who believes in the message presented in my first book "Unlocking Yes". In the fall of 2015 Tamer and I met in a downtown Toronto restaurant to discuss sales negotiation and sales prospecting for entrepreneurs. Tamer challenged me to dig deeper to develop a book designed specifically for the important and growing entrepreneurial market.

I dedicate *Perpetual Hunger* to my good friend and champion Tamer Hegazy for his insight and encouragement. To all of the entrepreneurial dreamers, risk takers and creators around the world…dream big. Dig deeper. Dare to be great!

CONTENTS

Patrick Tinney

INTRODUCTION

Sales prospecting is sustenance for any business, where growth is required and account turnover is nothing more than a fact of life. Sales prospecting is the precursor to consultative selling and sales negotiation. These three sales disciplines are permanently bolted together and reliant on each other. No company owns a piece of business in our 24/7 global world of unrelenting competition.

If you are reading this book, you are seeking constructive methods to dig new money out of the ground and guide this new found cash to profitable closure. In *"Perpetual Hunger: Sales Prospecting Lessons & Strategy"*, we offer a series of real-life experiences, business vignettes, tactics, lessons and strategies to help the reader make solid decisions to consistently prospect at a superior level. I like to call this "chasing smart money".

I have specifically written *Perpetual Hunger* to address the prospecting and account churn needs of sales professionals, entrepreneurs and start-ups. My mission is to provide you with strong examples of how to engage professional buyers who are well-schooled in procurement processes. Processes that are systematic and culturally designed to unbundle seller costs. *Perpetual Hunger* will enable sales professionals and entrepreneurs to bring their best sales game to any buyer's boardroom table.

As a sales prospector with a long career in sales, I am always in a state of perpetual sales hunger. My hunger for bigger and better customer opportunities will never diminish.

I seek out great customers and match them up with unique solutions to help make their businesses grow. It's about selling long-term value to new customers. My focus is that unique business solutions must provide a gateway to profitability in a measurable period of time for both our prospective customers and our enterprise alike.

Perpetual Hunger will do its best to be a long-term compass and reference for sales prospectors across the widest array of business categories. We will discuss and illustrate sales prospecting as an end-to-end thought process that is a gateway to successful consultative selling and sales negotiation closure.

Patrick Tinney

Your customers are professional buyers. Let's work together in *Perpetual Hunger* to reveal the information you need to develop into an accomplished, profitable sales prospector. Be a prospector who is prepared to intelligently engage the best procurement and buying professionals in your sales category.

Perpetual Hunger is written sequentially in lesson format to provide context to the exciting process of sales prospecting. I have inserted references to consultative selling and sales negotiation into *Perpetual Hunger* to give the reader and user a reference to the bigger sales picture. I have also added 12 game-changing exercises and a modest selection of sales negotiation strategies at the end of *Perpetual Hunger*. I did this to give new sales prospectors all the ammunition they need to close deals at any point in their sales hunt, for big game accounts.

As you read through *Perpetual Hunger* make notes. Complete the exercises. Practice makes perfect. Look for the lessons within this book that you can incorporate into your sales prospecting hunt right away.

On occasion, I have prefaced and repeated an exercise description as a reminder of the purpose of the exercise that follows. I did this so that you can focus on the exercise and avoid having to refer back to the lesson. This saves you time.

Please remember as you read *Perpetual Hunger* that all skill sets detailed within this book are scalable up or down to match any size of sales prospecting target accounts. All new sales are important and deserve your best skill sets and focus.

I'm pleased to share these sales prospecting lessons and sales prospecting strategies with you.

Here's to bountiful, big game, account hunting. Here's to profitability. Here's to a wonderful life of successful, perpetual sales hunger.

PART 1
PHILOSOPHY

Patrick Tinney

1

TODAY'S SALES PROSPECTING BIG GAME HUNT

We are eight years into the Great Recession and sales prospecting has never been more important.

Today, we stand with unprecedented consumer debt in North America. The USA is still bouncing in and out of recession-like economic conditions. The US Federal Reserve Bankers are so data dependent regarding the sluggish world economy that they choose not to raise interest rates. It is estimated that there is as much as $1.8 trillion dollars of unspent capital expenditure budgets lying dormant on North American corporate balance sheets. Corporations want to make money but do not want to spend money. Many businesses have resorted to shrinking the size of their operations to fit their declining revenues. Topline sales growth is a guessing game for many companies. Account churn is a challenge.

There are signs of economic improvement, but it's masked by the trillions of dollars of government Central Bank liquidity and quantitative easing being injected into financial systems around the world. Japan has even resorted to negative interest rates to encourage business growth.

Patrick Tinney

Sales prospecting is extremely competitive with too many sellers chasing too few buyers. This indicates we are in the clutches of a buyers' market, and the buyers know they have the upper hand. Question? What is your company doing to grow its topline sales and protect precious margins in this hunting expedition?

Business leaders have created a time compressed business world. Improved technology (both good and bad) and a 24/7 environment, means greater demands are placed on all business people. It doesn't matter whether you are selling or buying. Vendors need to sell more, while buyers need to take more time to research, consider and decide on their best options. As such, time compression reveals a fairly noticeable drop in civility. With so little time and so many changes in our current marketplace, we need to raise our game or have a competitor eat our sales breakfast.

Quickly add in the unique nature of your own company's competitive and economic realities, and now you *really* get the picture. In spite of all this, I am very constructive on sales prospecting and, I see opportunity everywhere.

As you read *Perpetual Hunger,* I want you to have a highlighter and a pen on hand. Write all over this book. Make notes and as I mentioned earlier, complete the exercises with the mindset that the personal learning and exploration of the exercises will significantly improve your sales prospecting skills. These are skills that will help you become a razor sharp business person. How will these exercises make me sharper you ask? It's simple. Skill sets you will be learning will be transferable to other segments of your business world.

Lastly, please approach Part I of *Perpetual Hunger* with an open mind. Part I is about philosophies around sales prospecting. Adopt the lessons and thought processes that resonate with you most. Pull these mind sets into your daily sales prospecting routines and grow your business. Having a philosophical base to fall back on will make sales prospecting more fun and doable. When the world of sales prospecting has order, backed by a solid philosophy, the only limits you face are the limits you yourself create. Let's start building our base. Let's get going!

2

YOU NEED A HUNGRY SALES PROSPECTING PHILOSOPHY

Sales prospecting is rough and tough. Anyone who has had to dig sales out of parched, hard earth knows it can be challenging to most and just too much for many. In my early days of selling community newspaper advertising in Edmonton, Alberta, I didn't own a car. My territory was many miles away from our office. Every morning, my roommate who also worked for the newspaper, would drive me out to the bottom end of my territory. I would be dressed in a three piece woolen, grey pin-stripe suit. It was a blistering hot summer and I would walk all day making cold calls on small businesses trying to sell advertisements into our newspaper. I would walk for miles to our designated pick up point for my ride back to the office, just in time to process my newly sold advertisements. This was my daily routine. Eventually, I wore out my only pair of dress shoes and had to write home to my mother to ask her for money for new shoes. All of my commissions were going to pay rent and to cover the numerous plates of French fries, gravy, beans and the occasional hamburger...the mainstay of my diet. Tough times. Regardless, these lessons made me humble and gritty. Later in my career, these tough times bolstered me when I had to dig deep, to close multi-million dollar deals.

I was totally focused on making dozens and dozens of physical cold calls or go hungry. Through these challenging times you develop a philosophy that drives you forward. Sales prospecting definitely requires a philosophy or a stacked base of hierarchical thinking to be your compass. Here is my five point philosophy for sales prospecting that will make you stronger and more importantly, make you money.

Customer churn is natural - In almost any market, there are customers who are entering and exiting. There are also customers who are restless and reallocating supplier expenditures in the market. This is natural and, to a degree healthy in that it keeps all sales professionals and entrepreneurs on their toes, searching for opportunities that are just around the corner. In my early days in business, we used to say if you see a truck stacked full of drywall…chase it, because it just might be heading to a new building with new customers.

Expect innovation and competition - The marketplace never rests on its past achievements, nor should you. The sheer mass and velocity of change in the market today is breathtaking. This always gives us something to talk about with new customers. We have a new story to share, to help their business become smarter, faster and more profitable with each new day. Our sales competitors feel exactly the same way, except, they never sleep. These competitors are always eyeing and maneuvering around our most prized accounts, hoping to show these customers their great new game changing ideas.

Build in a "No" factor - Not everyone is as enlightened as we are about our business point of difference. Not everyone has budget to participate in our great offers. Not everyone is going to like us. Too bad. The opportunity is that the above conditions change on an hourly and daily basis depending on our potential customer's needs. As a nine year old boy with a need for money after my dad suddenly passed away, I became obsessed with making money. My family was broke. Living in Canada, I decided to open up my own snow shoveling business and prayed for snow every day. If over an inch of snow fell, I was out after school and on weekends knocking on hundreds and hundreds of doors selling my snow shoveling services. Was I nervous about knocking on the door of a householder I didn't know? Not a chance. To me these homeowners were gold and I needed to work, so I could keep up with school activities that required money all the while taking financial pressure off my Mom. I was on a mission!

Hard work promotes prosperity - James Dyson, inventor of Dyson vacuum cleaners has built a multi-billion dollar business. Dyson built thousands of vacuum prototypes before finally meeting the expectations and needs of a hungry market. He did this with his own money in his own workshop. It took more than five years to get his Dyson model right but he had a vision and he wasn't going to give up without exhausting all technical avenues before achieving breakthrough success. Not all of us have years to stick with one dream. Today our Dyson vacuum cleaner friend owns his Dyson Ltd. multi-billion dollar business. Think about what you could own if you just worked a little harder and were a little more tenacious and innovative.

Get going! Stay hungry! - Get up and go. Being in a state of constant hunger is a goal driven mindset. As a precocious, young college student in Hamilton, Canada, I had a falling out with a lead instructor in my College Advertising Program. I was asked to leave and, I did. Sheridan College in Oakville, Ontario was the only other College that offered the same type of Advertising Program. Oakville was some 20 miles away from my home. There was another catch. The College program ran right through our frigid Canadian winters and I didn't own a car. Solution. Get up at 6 am every day. Eat as much breakfast as fast as I could and take two buses across Hamilton to the Queen Elizabeth Highway connecting Hamilton to Oakville and then hitchhike the remainder of the way to campus. I would stick out my thumb on the highway ramp and look every driver coming toward me straight in the eye. I hitchhiked to College every day and never missed a day of classes. I was never late. I graduated winning the prestigious T. Eaton Advertising award. Get going. Stay Hungry!

There is an old saying, *"If you give a person a fish, they will eat. If you teach a person to fish, they will eat for life."* Stay hungry and learn how to hunt and fish!

Patrick Tinney

3

FIVE KEY QUESTIONS IN SALES PROSPECTING

"Know thyself"…is an ancient Greek aphorism. This pithy saying is the basis for giving high achievers in sales prospecting a big advantage over their peers.

For context "we" is our company and our products. The party known as "they" is the customer "we" want to engage.

Dissect these five key sales prospecting questions.

1. Who are we?
2. Who are they?
3. Who do they think we are?
4. How do we find them?
5. How do we convince them…to need us?

The notion that "we" as a corporation send salespeople out into the business world without a deep understanding of what it is we are looking for can easily be described as lost productivity and wasted energy. Equally important is to understand what "we" (our brand) stands for in our market vertical.

1.   **Who are we?**

When a salesperson engages a potential new customer, the customer wants to know what our company name represents, what promises it makes and what promises it has kept with the products it sells. Customers also want to know how long, how consistently and how successfully our company has kept its brand promises.

A deep understanding of "we" information allows salespeople that represent our company to capably and persuasively describe who 'we' are. If you cannot describe who "we" are, how are you going to know if you are doing the best job selling your company's products?

One of the easiest ways for a customer to know if a salesperson understands their company and its products is to ask them to describe what they do in a sentence or two. If this short "elevator speech" is not compelling, it is unlikely the salesperson's proposal will be either.

2.   **Who are they?**

"They" are all that really matters. They are the customers for the products we sell. When we sell to a customer successfully over and over again, it is a form of confirmation. The customer needs or thinks they need our product and that we are doing a very good job communicating how our products will improve the customer's life. Our products make them feel confident and secure about the products they have purchased from us.

3.   **Who do they think we are?**

Who "they" think "we" are, is absolutely key. If customers identify with our company branding and promises, they will be more inclined to make our products part of their lives. If customers identify with the lifestyle our products represent, they will have no difficulty describing this to their friends and peers. If the customer identifies with the salesperson who sells our product because this salesperson exemplifies the lifestyle our products represent, there is a good chance this salesperson will sell more. This circular identification and affinity the customer has with our brand means we are doing a remarkable job of living our brand. If this circular "they to we" identification affinity builds, so does the brand and so does the brand's chance of hitting a cultural tipping point.

4.   **How do we find (they) them?**

Once we are able to clearly articulate our company's promises, we really only need to rank on a scale of one to five who our ideal customer is most likely to be. This exercise is the same if the customer target is B2B or B2C. Finding them begins with us. The more evangelical we are about this approach, the more successful we will become as prospectors and salespeople.

Years ago, when I worked in the newspaper flyer category business, I had a conversation with a colleague of mine, Paul Brown. Paul was the Advertising Director at The Observer, a Sarnia, Ontario newspaper. He said, *"Pat... we only drink coffee where our customers are."* On Friday's, in Sarnia, Paul would leave the office with a mapped plan to make calls on all of The Observer flyer customers and prospective new customers he could with his sales team.

So evangelical was this weekly sales practice that, when out on the road, coffee breaks were only taken in a customer cafeteria or at the snack counter. This truly exemplifies knowing your product so well you actually want to go out and chase customers down. You do this to make yourself and your brand so top of mind that when opportunities arise you are the first on the scene. This is truly living the brand. Paul identified with his customers so well, he knew them on a first name basis. The Observer customers knew Paul went out of his way to keep his company's promises. Paul and The Observer sales team took majority market share in a few short years from its flyer competitor. They ranked the customers they wanted and then flagged them down with their disciplined approach to The Observer brand.

Paul Brown has since left The Observer and has embraced entrepreneurism. Paul is now co-owner and Sales Manager of The Sarnia Journal, a start-up independent newspaper. Paul Brown exemplifies *Perpetual Hunger.*

5.   **How do we convince them...they need us?**

Since we started with five key questions, we will end with five more. We convince customers they need us by having them embrace our brand. We convince our customers by observing five points that create and maintain relevance in the customers mind.

1.   Does the customer have a need or perceived need we can fill?
2.   Does our product represent real or perceived value to the customer?

3. Have our brands, and the promises they represent been positively and consistently delivered to the market place?
4. Do we follow up with our customers to ask them if they are happy?
5. Are we constantly trying to anticipate our customer's needs?

4

WHY SALES PROSPECTING INTEGRATES WITH CONSULTATIVE SELLING

Sales prospectors are always looking for more effective ways to grow new relationships with important new customers. Gone are the days when a salesperson could just pick up the phone and get a quick appointment. Strong referrals from key customers are important.

Increasingly, customers are barricading themselves behind gatekeepers and virtual e-mail walls. Customers are only inviting into their inner circle, suppliers with whom they have a history or in whom they see great potential. On this note, a strong customer referral is essential for sellers who have to get over wide moats and thick walls. In this context, I believe consultative selling, trust, collaboration, and referrals are all connected when sales prospecting new clients.

Consultative selling helps to maintain margins through perceived and real demand for a seller's products. This is accomplished with an intimate understanding of the customer's business and category.

Consultative selling integrates nicely with referral based sales prospecting in the following ways:

1.   **Customers want creative ideas & solutions**

Suppliers who offer ideas that either save the customer money or potentially grow sales will be invited to the revenue expenditure planning party. A salesperson who consistently brings creative ideas/solutions to their customer's attention will be first in line.

With sales prospecting and consultative selling, the salesperson who is thinking creatively understands and anticipates the customer's appetite for risk. As a result, these trusted salespeople will have greater access to direct customer conversations to present ideas that will convert into revenue opportunities.

It is important to note, our customers want to shine in front of their peers and their company superiors. If a customer has a germ of an idea and wants to collaborate with a key supplier in search of a finished solution, new salespeople who are creative and consultative will be contacted more frequently.

2.   **Customers and trust**

Trust between two people is very personal. Consultative salespeople strive to hone and improve their trusted relationships with key customers. The importance of trust between a salesperson and the customer cannot be underestimated.

A former Director of Media Procurement for The Hudson's Bay Company once told me trust was what separated the people who won deals with him versus those who didn't. He indicated that on a weekly basis, many proposals were forwarded to him, all with compelling offers and value equations. When it came to choosing which deals to accept, he always asked himself, *"Which salespeople do I trust the most?"* These were the salespeople who won the deals and the people he relied on to execute professionally.

3.   **Sales prospectors who think consultatively move up the food chain**

As a salesperson, if you are not in the first or second call position with your important customers, selling will likely be more expensive. Sales prospectors who think consultatively understand that if they are in the third or lower call position they will be forced to sell at lower prices. This means these third and lower position salespeople are at greater risk of having their products commoditized by the customer. It also forces these same salespeople to buy market share to stay at the table with important customers.

Patrick Tinney

4.   **Selling one of anything is just plain expensive**

With the rising "cost of sale", why would sales management go to the expense of selling just one of anything to a customer?

Sales prospecting from a consultative perspective encourages both buyers and sellers to look for more common ground. Everyone benefits when both parties realize that a consultative sales relationship is based on trust, good value, collaboration, and a long-term view of the market.

An advanced proposition is to raise the sales prospecting bar in your sales organization with an integrated consultative sales backdrop. This means we want new customers and we want longer, even generational, relationships.

5

SALES PROSPECTORS MUST DEFINE NEW CUSTOMERS

Having spent my career in the corporate world with access to great national research and analytics, I was always aware of my primary market. It was pretty easy. In many cases, finding new money was market driven by businesses making plans to open up offices or retail outlets in Canada. These expansion plans were reasonably easy to predict or ferret out. To that point, I used to take one day out of all my vacations to the southern USA and do store checks, to get ahead of the market. It was a hunting expedition. Some of the store brands were so new I couldn't predict whether or not they would expand to Canada. In other cases, there were whispers from the press or from the retail market place that retail competitors were on the way.

Before heading to Florida for vacation one year, I had heard a rumor that Lowes Home Renovation was preparing to expand into Canada to take on Home Depot, who had landed here years earlier. I made a point of dropping into a Florida Lowes store and was really interested in how its store layout, signage and merchandise differed from Home Depot. I found myself walking around the store staring up at the signage when, out the corner of my eye, I saw a man watching me. He approached me and asked what I was doing looking up. I identified myself as working for The Hollinger Newspaper Group and confided I had information suggesting Lowes was planning to open up locations in Canada shortly. He identified himself as the Store Manager. His eyes widened on my research. He had just moved to Florida from New York State where he was part of the planning team charged with the preparation to set up shop in Canada. With that, the conversation became very warm. He knew I meant no harm in studying his store and he proceeded to take me on a personal tour. He willingly shared key insights with explanations of Lowes key leverage points and the challenges within his market.

Wow, did my ritual of doing store checks on vacation ever pay off? When I returned to my Toronto office with all of this new intelligence, we were clearly way ahead of our media competitors.

When preparing to write my first book "Unlocking Yes" I approached seasoned daily newspaper editor and book author David Kingsmill and asked him for a couple of pointers on preparing to write a book. David's advice was sage. He said 'Pat, you must always write for a targeted market. If you do not write for a specific market you will stray off course and get bogged down'. What a wonderful gift David gave me. David's navigation put me on course. I focused my writing targeted to sales professionals and sales managers. It later turned out that sales entrepreneurs would emerge as a third key market.

The above information leads us to ask important questions of our target markets when we are sales prospecting.

1. What is our primary market and customer profile?
2. What is our secondary market and customer profile?
3. Where do we find these unique customers?
4. What research can we leverage to sharpen our identification of our intended markets?
5. How will these customer segments identify with our product offerings?

These are all vital questions and really must be answered before we even make our first official calls to prospective clients. Otherwise, we are burning cash while looking for a needle in a haystack.

I also recommend ranking the revenue mass and profitability of potential prospective accounts so you stay totally focused on "chasing smart money".

A.   Rank your primary and secondary business categories on a scale of 1 to 5 based on the potential dollar expenditure you estimate is available.

B.   Rank your primary and secondary accounts on a scale of 1 to 5 based on the potential budget expenditures you believe there is in each account in these business categories.

This ranking exercise will really focus your efforts in sales prospecting and in strategy, when asked to prepare budgets for your sales prospecting plan. All of the above information, ranking and data collection are much needed. Once compiled, we can start to ask these really intelligent questions.

1. Which business categories and accounts must we acquire as game-changers to our sales prospecting efforts?
2. What unique offerings and price will we have to present in order to secure these game-changing accounts?
3. Which accounts are "bell weather" accounts that need to be prospected immediately knowing other accounts in that business category follow their moves in a herd mentality?

My final pieces of advice are to stay strategic in your overall sale prospecting plan. Develop a plan of attack and stay with it. It will be your roadmap and compass. From a tactical perspective chase smart money. By this I mean, chase accounts that are active and spending in your business space. Make special notes and call for assistance from any navigators and friends that you have working in or with these target account companies.

EXERCISE 1 — DEFINING NEW CUSTOMERS

I have been through some monster sales prospecting efforts over my career combing industry lists and databases. I can tell you that you must break down sales prospecting data and rank it. You do this to stay focused and proceed with confidence.

A.   What are the top three ranked primary business categories you must prospect?

1. _____

2. _____

3. _____

B.   What are the top 10 accounts across the above categories you must prospect?

1. _____

2. _____

3. _____

4. _____

5. _____

6. _____

7. _____

8. _____

9. _____

10. _____

6

FIVE WAYS TO JUMPSTART SALES PROSPECTING SUCCESS

As a salesperson who pounded a lot of pavement over the years, I developed a set of thought processes I believe made me more money than many of my colleagues, especially when it came to sales prospecting.

This started as a young boy. I took every job I could think of as long as it was legal. This meant I knocked on hundreds and hundreds of doors while refining my pitch in order to close deals faster and more consistently.

After my college days, I was drawn through the community newspaper system by a bunch of gnarly former Thomson Newspaper professionals. These sales grinders used every trick in the book to meet new customers and drive revenue.

Both of the above events prepared me to make juicy commission checks. This hands-on learning taught me to think of sales prospecting as a discipline, not some "You have to earn your stripes drudgery." I looked at my sales prospecting skills as a craft and I got totally annoyed with myself if I blew a call. To point, I can still remember that last time I mucked up a call, pitching a customer for business in my daily newspaper days. That call still haunts me. I knew I was much better than my performance revealed. I knew that I participated in a call without enough work-up and without the right tools. Don't let this happen to you.

Patrick Tinney

Here are five mental exercises and tools to jumpstart your sales prospecting success.

1.   **Preparation** - Back in 1979 at a community newspaper in Oakville, Canada, our Sales Manager would occasionally hold brief case checks. He conducted these surprise checks before we left the office in the morning to go prospecting for new customers. Heaven help you, if you did not have all of the sales tools in your briefcase to close deals on the spot with new advertisers. Flash forward to today. Has anything changed? Yes and no. Yes, I can pull up my company's website and show potential customers tons of data and client testimonials. Data that shows what we are doing to create a competitor crushing point of difference. No, things have not changed, I still need to get the customer excited and involved in what I am selling. I do this with all kinds of brilliant visuals and creative material designed to place questions in the customer's mind. What huge business opportunity is he/she missing out on if they do not buy my product immediately? This preparation allows me to deliver a great elevator speech accompanied by a set of benefits on steroids. Plus, it allows me to add value statements to make the customer feel assured, I make the customer's life smarter, faster, better and safer. This is what I hope to achieve in our first meeting.

2.   **Anticipate needs** - If we are listening very closely to our prospective customer, we can start to visualize how we can add great value to the customer's world, fostering a longer term relationship. We search our eco-system of products and services. We bring forward creative ideas to the customer to set our company apart from our competitors. We do this to help our customer grow revenue in ways they may not have otherwise anticipated.

3.   **Succeed with deeds** - Alert sales professionals have a tendency to consistently over-deliver. These same sales professionals show up and make sure the customer just loves the new experience with their products and services. If, for whatever reason, our first product execution is not perfect, we are there with the customer. We stand by the customer to assure her we will smooth out any problems that are just part of the transition period for both of our companies. We go out of our way to make it right with new customers. After all, we are building trust and a longer term relationship where everyone wins and is profitable.

4.   **Embrace positive risk** - If you want to hit a homerun in business you had better get used to the idea of embracing positive risk. Positive risk is what sets the big money winners apart from the "Steady Eddie" types of the world. If you want

22

to make big revenue bonus payouts you have to be smarter, faster and more creative than your cohorts. You have to show up and help your customer when your bright ideas are not perfect on delivery. Is this risky? Not really. Is it risky to play it safe every day and hope for the best? If your customers do not see you as a cutting edge supplier, you will be reduced to a commodity and cast aside into a heap of also ran sales professionals.

5.   **Factor in No's** - Let's go back to the youngster at the beginning of this discussion. This little boy was determined not to fail. Failing was not an option. "No's" are a part of life. No's must be accepted when we run out of great arguments to buy our product. The youngster just looked at "no's" as a natural part of life. I didn't even think I was selling in those days. I had a vital product to offer. It was my advanced view of the business world. How could anyone resist my offer to work hard for them? Bring the youngster back into your mind as you sales prospect and factor in the no's. It's part of sales prospecting. The no's actually help you work on your objection handling skills. No's are actually positive over time.

Question? How are you going to jump start your sales prospecting success?

Patrick Tinney

7

THREE BRIDGES TO ENTREPRENEURIAL SALES PROSPECTING

When we engage new prospective customers, the first thought that comes to mind is, how are we going to bridge the gap between our business world and theirs? After all, we are strangers. We don't know each other's likes, dislikes and tender points. We don't know about each other's values and integrity standards.

Having acknowledged the above, we do know that all of us in business have three bridges that must be built in order to conduct business successfully and profitably.

1.   **Question bridges -** I could write a small book about the importance of questions. Armor piercing questions help us understand our prospective customer's goals, objectives, motives, fears, aspirations and achievements. Wisely crafted questions signal to our prospective customers that we are approaching them with humility and have their interests at heart. Great questions signal to customers that we have researched their business even before entering into a conversation with them. Therefore, we are asking intelligent questions directed at seasoned buyers. Sharp questions set the table for strong relationships. A great opening question I often use with new customers is *"What opportunity do you see*

in your business that is vitally important to your growth that you are unable to reach with your current knowledge and resources?"

2.   **Relationship bridges** - To bring two business partners together, we must establish trust in a low self-interest manner as quickly as possible. As I often tell participants in our Centroid Training sessions "If you have not built a bridge to your customers, you had better enjoy swimming." Clearly, understanding and empathizing with a potential customer's needs, wants, strengths, weakness and exposure, positions us to approach them with customized ideas and solutions for problems they may be experiencing. This is especially so regarding problems they have not even fully appraised. By opening up our business world to them in a way that makes our potential customers smarter, faster, better and more profitable, we are building a bridge. It's a strong bridge to a wonderful, long-term collaborative, trust based relationship. In this light, we see our potential new customers as potential friends. Friends who will recommend our work. Friends who will promote us in their trusted relationship family and business networks. In many cases, the profound quality of our relationship has the potential to build a bond that will last a lifetime.

3.   **Promise bridges** - The minute we engage a new prospective customer, they and we are making decisions about each other's potential promises we both expect will be kept. Promise bridges are comprised of three main pillars.

First, we as salespeople are walking promises. The way we dress, groom, speak, listen and query all add up to a set of promises. The way we solve problems and deliver value, beyond what was called for is another promise. The most important personal promise is our integrity promise. This is what I call "the show up promise". When problems arise in business, we show up and fix them as quickly as possible to keep all customer systems moving smoothly and effortlessly.

The second promise pillar is the value we bring to the table in every engagement with our prospective customers. Value can be expressed in many different ways. I believe true value is our ability to be a long-term partner for our customers. In this role, we are constantly anticipating our customer's needs and trying to solve their problems. Sometimes, even before they even realize they have a problem. It is the way long-term friends relate to one another. It is the value our customers place on our sound judgement and advice as a trusted insider.

The last promise pillar is the promises our company makes and keeps flawlessly on an everyday basis. This is called brand. In my humble opinion, new customers buy salespeople first, value second and brand third. This is how we establish the slow confident walk across the promise bridge to business relationships, mutual profitability and deals signed to last a lifetime.

So, to my entrepreneurial sales prospectors, make this the year of building bridges with new prospective customers. Do this so you both profit and grow exponentially. Remember, build smart question bridges. Build sturdy relationship bridges, and, build promise bridges that stabilize and strengthen these relationships with each passing day.

8

SALES PROSPECTORS PRODUCT POINT OF DIFFERENCE IS KEY

With all of the intense competition for buyer's budget expenditures, our product point of difference (POD) stands out as one of the leading indicators of our ability as sales prospectors to rise above the competition.

Let's face it, if all we are offering in the market is another product in a sea of mediocrity then, our product offering immediately sinks to a commoditized discussion with the client. This all ends badly with the client scratching his/her head wondering why they would ever consider changing from a current supplier to us. This leads to an unsavory discussion about price compression.

Our expression of company and product brand value immediately comes to the fore. This is closely followed by an explanation of our uniqueness in our product space.

In order to properly position our company and product POD, I believe a sales prospector must be able to address the following topics about their offerings effortlessly.

1.   **Corporate brand** - Brand is simply a collection of perfectly executed promises that happen daily and hourly. When I think of great brands with longevity that get our immediate attention, I think of Pepsi Co., Molson-Coors, The PGA of America to mention a few. All have great stories of growth, resilience and success. Brands such as Google, Facebook and Apple are three new juggernaut brands. When a representative from one of these companies contacts a prospective client there is a cachet attached to these brands and chances are the client will return the call. Therefore, the question is where does your company rank in its business vertical and what is its POD?

2.   **Execution of brand** - I could talk for hours about brand execution. This has so much to do with how we meet customer expectations every time they engage our company. It speaks to how Fortune 500 companies respond to great challenges or opportunities with its customer base. In my view, Apple is doing such a great job in the area of brand execution, I think everyone else in the space is just trying to keep up with them. In the retail space, I like what Indigo Book Stores are doing in Canada. Indigo totally retooled its outlets to become a destination lifestyle store for books, music, toys and gifts. Combining the aforementioned with a great online offering creates a brilliant extension of the brand.

3.   **Market share** - It is hard to ignore a market leader. In my days with a leading newspaper, customers were compelled to speak to us because we had the best daily print channel to reach their customer base. How is your company positioning your market share with prospective customers? Knowing how your company ranks relative to market share and the importance your prospective customer places on this metric is critical in sales prospecting. This is another angle of POD.

4.   **Customer loyalty** - When approaching new customers, it is impressive to say, *"Our customers are so loyal; they will go to extraordinary lengths to get our product and use it in ways that continue to amaze us."* Campbell's Soup and Old Bay Spice immediately come to mind. What is the POD of your company customer loyalty and how can you use this information to constructively influence new clients to buy your product?

5.   **Product innovation** - We now live in a world that is constantly disrupting old rules while embracing a myriad of new technology and innovation. Customers love innovative thinking because if they can embrace this new thinking first, it just might give them a leg up on their competitors. How is your company innovating

and how can you express this as a POD that will make your customer's life safer, smarter faster and better?

6.   **Product pipeline** - Any company that wants to keep its customer base engaged and full of anticipation has to have great ideas and innovations in its product pipeline. Companies that have a great reputation for idea generation get our greatest attention and exhibit their POD.

7.   **Product reliability** - When thinking about changing from one supplier to another, customers really focus on product reliability. If we are selling a business-to-business product that must integrate into the customer's operation, the customer wants the lowest exposure possible. They want products to show up and work as hard as they do. Customers also want to know, if they are experiencing any challenges or slowing of daily operations as a result of switching to our product, that we will be there to trouble shoot with the customer. This may mean staying on site or travelling to a global operation until everything is running smoothly. Ensure you deliver your POD every step of the way as promised. Large customers do not suffer poor product or service reliability easily.

Ultimately, POD may be one of those topics you might want to cover in an elevator speech. It may require us as sales prospectors who are trying to land monster accounts to be able to articulate our POD with fabulous key leverage points. It may also have a great deal to do with our prospective customer looking at us and saying, *"I know that making the switch to your company is a great decision because I know you will show up rain or shine."*

Patrick Tinney

EXERCISE 2 — POINT OF DIFFERENCE

With all of the intense competition for buyer's budget expenditures, our product point of difference (POD) stands out as one of the leading indicators of our ability as sales professionals to rise above the competition.

Now think about what sets you apart from your competition. Write all possible constructive points of difference. Finally, rank your top five product points of difference.

1. _____
   _____
   _____

2. _____
   _____
   _____

3. _____
   _____
   _____

4. _____
   _____
   _____

5. _____
   _____
   _____

9

TIPS ON HOW TO BUILD AN EFFECTIVE ELEVATOR SPEECH

I am absolutely amazed at just how many sales and senior executives do not have an effective elevator speech.

In the truest sense, an elevator speech is a summation of what it is that you offer as a sales professional in about 30 seconds or less. Thirty seconds is about how long it takes to travel between floors in an office building, thus the name elevator speech.

You might ask, why do I need to bother with an elevator speech, especially, if you work for a nationally branded company and you have a huge title that resides on a glossy business card? You dress like a Wall Street executive and you have all of the confidence of a person who is making it big time. Of course prospective clients will want to talk to you.

Sorry, the above just does not cut it. None of us can be assured we will be of interest to a prospective new client based on a business card with a widely recognizable corporate brand.

I can remember working with one particular senior executive on his elevator speech. He was preparing to take his business to the next level and expand his client base internationally. When discussing the need for an elevator speech with him, I could see a quizzical, almost furrowed expression on his face. So, I said to him, *"Please stand up next to me. Now visualize that you are at a soccer field with your niece very early on a Saturday."* I asked him to turn his back to me. I purposely backed into him and turned around to apologize. I said, *"Sorry, I didn't see you there. Hi my name is Joe and I am the Chief Financial Officer of XYZ Global Accounting Inc. What do you do?"* Unprepared with an elevator speech, my client was at a loss for words. He immediately understood the need for a polished elevator speech. He understood that this chance meeting with the CFO might never happen again and he had the opportunity of a lifetime, if he could just get the right words out calmly and naturally.

It is worth noting, if you are the CEO of a multi-national corporation, your title alone carries great gravitas. Notwithstanding, you may still want to have a backup elevator speech for interactions out of your business category and if you are pursuing non-conventional business.

I have worked with many senior executives and business owners on their elevator speeches. I am always delighted when they finally discover how to articulate their unique self and point of difference in a few words.

I know I have struck gold when working with someone on building their elevator speech when they suddenly say "Stop! What did you just say there? Can you please slow down and please repeat that?"

A really good elevator speech has nothing to do with the name of our business. When I start to work with executives on their speech, I ask them what they do. Inevitably they start off saying, *"I work for and I am…"* My response is always the same. I say, *"SO WHAT. There are hundreds of suppliers just like you in the market."* Some clients just stare at me blankly. Others get red faced. The alert ones say, *"I get it. We need to start working on this right now."* A great elevator speech has everything to do with the value and promises you idealize on a daily basis. An elevator speech must contain the unique benefits you bring to any business partner. We want them to believe that engaging you will help make them smarter, faster, better or profitable.

What is Patrick Tinney's elevator speech you ask? "I help businesses make and save money." This elevator speech is begging the question…. *"HOW?"*

You want people to query your elevator speech to allow you to open a conversation with them. This allows us to reciprocate and ask questions about their world and business.

Patrick Tinney's elevator speech may be one of the shortest in history. So let's say you work for a financial services company where you sell stocks, bonds and mutual funds to consumers. A simple elevator speech for you might be, *"I help hard working people grow and maximize personal wealth in a manner that lowers risk in any financial market conditions."* Again, we are back to the customer who asks, *"How do you do that?"* or *"I'd like to hear more about how you do that."*

Now, sales professionals and entrepreneurs, work hard on your elevator speech. Write several versions of it. Practice it on your family, friends and business colleagues. You will know when you've got it right when people start asking you how you just did that. This is exactly when you know you are on the way to raising your sales prospecting game to a new level. It's a wondrous level that anticipates and relishes the opportunity to bump into a "once in a lifetime client opportunity".

EXERCISE 3 — A GREAT ELEVATOR SPEECH

This is important and worth repeating.

A great elevator speech has everything to do with the value and promises you idealize on a daily basis. An elevator speech must contain the unique benefits you bring to any business partner. In a way it makes them believe engaging with you could help make them smarter, faster, better or profitable.

What is Patrick Tinney's elevator speech you ask? *"I help businesses make and save money"*. This elevator speech is begging the question.... *"HOW?"*

So let's say you work for a financial services company where you sell stocks, bonds and mutual funds to consumers. A simple elevator speech for you might be *"I help hard working people grow and maximize personal wealth in a manner that lowers risk in any financial market conditions."*

Now write your elevator speech. Write several versions until it is focused, believable and natural.

1. _____
   _____
   _____
   _____

2. _____
   _____
   _____
   _____

3. _____
   _____
   _____
   _____

10

TEN WINNING PROSPECTING TRAITS

The very best sales prospectors are high achievers. They exhibit a unique set of qualities and tendencies that many of us just do not exhibit.

Some of the most successful sales prospectors I have ever had the pleasure to work with, approach potential customers as if they are on a mission they expect to win.

Great sales prospectors are comprised of a balance IQ and EQ that is insidious and resourceful.

The very best sales prospectors are naturally gifted or have mastered varying combinations of the following traits.

Can you imagine someone with a great product or service to sell who is gifted with all of the following traits?   The word "magnificent" comes to mind!

Hunger - Living in a perpetual state of hunger is a way of thinking that not everyone possesses. Some of us are hungry for the great satisfaction of closing a piece of business. Others of us have short bursts of hunger in closing out on new business. Then we become satisfied and pull back. The very best sales prospectors are so hungry for new business that this thought process fills their mind until it is time to stop, and not before.

Inquisitiveness - By nature, sales prospectors with inquisitive minds are able ask money questions while thinking ahead to the next question well before a prospective customer has answered their first query. They are mental data miners who masterfully use open ended questions. As a result the inquisitive minded person is quickly and concisely getting to the root of the new customer's needs, demands and wants.

Tactical - Tactical thinkers see sales prospecting as a theatre of the mind. They quickly assess the other side's strengths and weakness. They devise routes of engagement with maneuvers and back up tactics to invite us into their business world. They capture our attention and entertain us while quietly closing routes of escape for their newest potential partner.

Analytic process - Here we have the number crunchers and the masters of logic. They induce outcomes and plans for deductive closure. Analytic thinkers bring out the beauty in numbers. They have the ability to simplify complicated equations designed to lull us into a state of openness and enjoyment of the buying experience.

Emotional intelligence - Rather than IQ it's EQ. It's a talent that helps you understand those around you without them saying much. Those with higher EQ detect body language, eye contact, change in mood and atmosphere. They sense the other side by reading the room. They have real empathy.

Creative agility - This is truly a great gift as it allows sales professionals to shift gears and instantly adapt to customer objections and new selling scenarios. Creative agility makes sales prospectors appear to be under whelmed by quick changes in direction from a potential customer. It gives professional sales prospectors the poise and confidence to stay grounded in the present. They tumble ideas until a deal is done or they feel this customer does not have the means to buy.

Discipline – Sales prospectors with great discipline know how to plan for a mission to close a sale with a new customer as quickly as possible. Disciplined sales prospectors always have a game plan. Their sales scripting and cost modeling are so well placed, they know exactly when to close. They neutralize the other side with their advance reconnaissance and smooth, relentless probing to uncover the moment of opportunity to get a "yes" from a customer.

Storytellers - Sales prospecting raconteurs set the stage for building trust and agreement with their ability to weave life changing benefits so that customers have a tough time resisting. They know how to prime the well. They add in anecdotal references to help the other side understand why they must act now or lose out on a great buying opportunity. Storytellers make us feel good and help buyers truly enjoy their purchases for years to come without a second thought.

Persistence - Sales prospectors who refer to themselves as persistent have one of the strongest qualities a salesperson can claim. It means they have a strong ability to accept the answer "no" from a customer. They take the "no" and qualify it as "*no I need more information*" or "*no I am not the right customer*". If the latter customer no is discovered, persistent sales prospectors take this as a small speed bump on route to the next customer who will say yes and accept closure of a sale. It is a mental state that suggests to the sales prospector that the only entity truly standing between them and success is their own mind. Persistence is found in all great sales prospectors.

Killer instinct - Those with killer instinct are not afraid to seize a moment in a prospective sale that may not appear again. They know that moment of truth when closing a quick sale will require an extra little nudge. This instinct is also about knowing when the other side is truly open and accepting. Sales prospectors with killer instinct know perseverance is just part of the sales prospecting process.

So here's a question to all sales managers out there. How does your sales team measure up with the above traits? And, how are you going to improve their skills? With training the above skills can be learned or improved exponentially.

11

Benefits On Steroids

Part of our work in sales prospecting is translating the data on our product into workable language that piques our customer's interest at just the right moment. There is a bit of mental baggage that comes with this concept for many of us in sales. We tend to talk about the product in technical or industry terms. We use industry jargon and acronyms. We assume everyone in the room understands what we, the experts, are talking about.

Now think of yourself as a time pressed customer who needs help to buy a new product or service that is outside of the normal work scope. What is it that you really want to hear when you as a customer are wedged into this confusing space? In short, you want to be able to explain what it is you are buying to your colleagues and friends so you don't look like you bought a big white elephant. Understandably, you don't want to find yourself bathing in buyer's remorse.

As a buyer, you want to acquire a greater understanding of this product. You want a confident feeling that you are smarter, faster, better, and that this product you are planning to purchase will improve your life. The product must make you feel that life will be more predictable, soothing, creative, and productive. Furthermore, we want it to be profitable. So how do we get this feeling if the person who is selling to us just talks about a bunch of product feature gibberish?

Now back to reality. Put your seller's hat back on and let's start selling features converted into "Benefits On Steroids".

Here are a couple of examples using my own sales training company www.centroidmarkting.com

Centroid Training Sales Pitch to prospective client.

Features -

1. *"Centroid Training offers a panoramic view of sales training from prospecting to consultative selling to sales negotiation housed under one roof."*
2. *"We have 30+ years of corporate sales, management and product development with large budget companies etched into our learning programs."*

Customer reaction might be... Yawn...big deal... who cares... boring. Unless, these features are followed up with:

Benefits on Steroids -

1. *"This means, you'll feel safer in knowing Centroid will listen to you and customize all aspects of your company sales training to alleviate your unique business pain points. This helps you realize quick ROI on your training investment. Furthermore, your sales team will meet or beat industry benchmark, sales standards."*
2. *"Which means to you, Centroid will work with your sales team to constructively change sales behaviors with deep content and field tested money making simulations. We will build your team's revenue growth skills and will not leave until the job is done. This is why our clients hire Centroid time and again."*

As you can see, benefits on steroids are simple to digest and are causality based using transition phrases to begin the benefit. In other words, they include features that are converted into smarter, faster, better, benefit statements, improving the customer's world. The customer can repeat or translate these benefits to their family and colleagues as if they were their own ideas.

Patrick Tinney

So, step back and think like a customer as you build your benefit statements. Wow your customer with easy to understand life changing, positive, benefits on steroids. Your customers will love you for it and will buy your products and services time and again.

EXERCISE 4 — BENEFITS ON STEROIDS

Great benefit statements are ones that simplify complicated features and turn them into life changing events that really get the customer excited. These statements are what I refer to as "Which means..." or "Meaning to you..." statements. These causality benefit statements must immediately resonate with the customer. They must be simple and they must build great word pictures in the customer's mind that can easily be repeated with great confidence and pride.

Here is a Centroid Training feature.

"We have 30+ years of corporate sales, management and product development with large budget companies etched into our learning programs"

Here is a Centroid Training benefit.

"Which means to you, Centroid will work with your sales team to constructively change sales behaviors with deep content and field tested money making simulations. We will build your teams revenue growth skills and will not leave until the job is done. This is why our clients hire Centroid time and again."

Now list two of your product features.

1._____

_____

2._____

_____

Now write two "Which means" or "Meaning to you" benefit statements. Remember to make them exciting life changing benefits. Think benefits on steroids.

1._____

_____

2._____

_____

12

ATTITUDE IS EVERYTHING IN COLD CALLING

As sales professionals we must cold call to replenish our customer base. Customers can and frequently do change their perspective on what is good for them and the future of their businesses. This movement is not personal. It tends to be more pragmatic and forward looking. Times change. Management groups change. Business categories go through reshaping processes. It's natural and Darwinian. The strong in business adapt and thrive.

Oddly enough, this is good for business as long as we, as business people, stay in touch with our market verticals and do not become entrenched in the good old days. Yes, they were good days but there are also great days ahead if we keep looking forward with an open and flexible business mindset.

All of what I am saying is exactly why cold calling is vital to business. We must keep searching for new markets and new customers with whom we can build bridges and collaborate on great business opportunities. In essence, we grow together. One can say it's an attitude or perspective. The way we approach new customers is also an attitude. As a sales professional, I rarely shied away from a conversation with a new customer. I always believed there was great opportunity if only we had the chance to talk openly about the customer's business opportunities

42

and aspirations. So, the next time you are gearing up to make a fresh set of cold calls stay open minded. Here are a few tips and observations to keep you in a positive frame of mind no matter what the outcome of the cold call.

1.   **A conversation** - A cold call is nothing more than the beginning of a conversation. Some conversations go well and a great bridge is built to prosperity and a lifelong business relationship. Other conversations just don't get on track. There can be 1001 reasons why you were unable to build a conversational bridge. Personal and/or business pressures can often get in the way. Don't be discouraged. If one conversation doesn't work, be confident that the next one will. It's all about our attitude.

2.   **Humility** - I am a great believer in steely confidence. I am also a believer in humility. If we are approaching a successful business person remember, it's all about them. They hold the keys to our future and success. A new customer does not owe us anything but a moment of his or her time. If we spend that moment with them wisely and empathetically, we may open a door to great wealth for both of us.

3.   **Their domain** - Whether we are cold calling a customer on the phone, via e-mail or best of all in person, we are entering their domain. It's their house. They create the rules until such time as we can show value and identify their immediate needs or profound wants. Respect the customer's home. They built it with great pride, perspiration and personal cost.

4.   **Elevator speech** - We must learn to make our 30 second elevator speech our second skin. A skin that is flexible. We want our elevator speech to be so internalized that, no matter how many times the customer interrupts us or knocks us off script, we can naturally rejoin our speech effortlessly, brimming with energy.

5.   **Questions** - When cold calling, prepare questions for the customer that are meaningful and full of constructive intent. Ask the customer about their business category and the progress they are making in their business. Ask them about their needs, hopes and future planning. You will be amazed what you get, if you give generously with well-crafted high value questions.

6.   **Their story** - The vast majority of people who run a business or have built a business from scratch have great pride in their work. Every business story is a unique story. Let's be honest, we all love to share our greatest successes, and on the odd occasion talk about the one (opportunity) that got away. If we as sales

professionals can tune into and channel this unique customer story, there is sure to be a treasure of customer information. This information that will open up needs and wants the customer has which they may have never thought deeply about.

7.   **Listening** - Believe it or not, the more we listen and encourage the customer to continue sharing their story, the more they like it. They begin to feel that we are connecting with their deepest thoughts. This builds trust. If the customer permits it, taking notes is wonderful because it adds another layer in connection and interest on our part. While listening, I love using what I call garbage language. I use encouraging language to keep the customer expanding their story. I use phrases such as *"No kidding." "How is that possible?" "Wow!" "Seriously?" "Holy Cow!" "How did it all end?"* These are all just prompts, but they work amazingly well and let the customer know that we are totally tuned into them.

8.   **Benefits on steroids** - When it is time for us to speak, make sure we demonstrate our product or service in a way that the customer immediately sees benefits in purchasing. I like to call them benefits on steroids. These benefits are so strong the customer sees a bright future doing business with us. The customer visualizes being smarter, faster, better, safer and more profitable. This is our moment to shine and pull the customer into our business world.

9.   **Trial close** - As a sales professional, I prefer to trial close to conclude a sale rather than hard closing. Why? The reason is, I can trial close all day long and never get knocked out of the potential for the sale, as long as I can keep the customer talking. An example of the trial close is "Who in your organization will benefit from our product the most?" It is such a simple question yet it demands a descriptive, thought provoking answer from the customer. They may even close the sale for us on the spot. They may realize that this group within their organization needs help and we (the cold caller) have arrived at just the right moment to assist them. I don't believe in wasting time. I believe in working smart. If I feel I have exhausted my best trial closes or if I believe the customer is just playing me for information, I have no hesitation in asking for a sale with a direct yes or no question. Remember, always work smart and work within your plan.

10.   **Post mortem** - After each cold call regardless whether it was a great experience or otherwise, take a moment and pause. Ask yourself, what did we do just now that was so compelling? Ask yourself what was the turning point that closed the sale or got us a product test? Conversely, if the cold call went poorly

re-play the call in your mind and ask yourself could we have saved this call? Or, was it just bad timing? Or, was it just one of those circumstances that were not going to work out any time in the near future. In this post mortem process, be your own best friend. There is no benefit in beating yourself up. There is wonderful learning in honest discourse with our inner self for constant improvement.

Finally, be brave and strong. It's a time tested winning attitude.

Patrick Tinney

13

ESTABLISHING CUSTOMER NEEDS

Let's be really honest. If a customer doesn't have a need for your product or service it is unlikely you will close a sale. Notwithstanding, we as sales professionals, have to dig into the customer's mind. We dig through a very thoughtful process to discern and rank what we believe to be the customer's needs.

Our questions have to be high value in order to get the customer to open up. Questions must be directed to reveal areas of their business needing their greatest attention. Once we have a ranking of these needs we can go about our job of looking for creative solutions involving our products and services based on our unique point of difference.

Customer high value questions could include:

1. Where are your competitors succeeding right now, where you would like to advance?
2. What product innovations in my business vertical interest you the most right now?
3. When customers speak to your sales representatives, what are their needs and how urgent are their needs?

46

4. If you could make one change in your business knowing it would drive sales velocity, what would it be?
5. What qualities do you look for in a long-term supplier?

The customer's response to these questions and questions like them will give us a ranked order of what the customer needs. Our point of difference, quality variables, delivery times and pricing will round out the picture for us as a studious sales prospector. This information propels us to produce an eye-popping proposal that will make the customer feel a strong and encouraging emotional attachment to our solutions. This attachment will make the customer feel smarter, faster, safer and better than their competitors.

In the event the customer feels that they have no perceived need for our product, then we must work harder to uncover a latent need or clearly illustrate a need of which they were not aware. We must create interest and intrigue. We have to appeal to the customer's aspirational needs and long-term goals.

One of my favorite questions in uncovering long-term goals and aspirations is to ask… "What vital business can you see that you cannot reach with your current resources and talent base?"

When the customer answers this question they will be uncovering their need to fill this gap. They will also be offering an indicator of how important this potential sales/revenue gap is to them and their future success.

I want to make a point of distinction here. Customers buy, based on needs first, especially, in our current, tight global buyers' market conditions. By this I mean we actually have too many sellers and not enough buyers. Therefore, the market is awash in products and short on cash. Customers in the corporate world feel safe about replacing worn out products but are reluctant to buy anything not producing an instant constructive result.

Wants can drive a customer to buy when they become verified by potential needs. For instance, if your company sells cyber security software most corporations will listen to you. Fear of security breaches has become so intense that needs and wants actually blend together to create an emotional hybrid need/want powerhouse. No company wants to be remembered as the one that had all of their customer data leaking all over the Internet or worse yet placed into criminal hands.

Work hard with potential customers. Uncover real needs, latent needs, aspirations and goals. Figure out where their revenue gaps are. Bring great awe inspiring ideas

Patrick Tinney

to your potential customers. Customers buy ideas. Customers buy products that offer them benefits on steroids. Customers buy from sellers who are genuinely interested in their business and look at business relationships in the longer term. This real interest on our part builds relationships. It also clarifies trust and integrity. As a seller, do your homework. Ask high value questions. Stay brave, bold and strong. This is how you uncover money making needs.

14

THE IMPORTANCE OF GOAL SETTING

In the process of goal setting there are two distinct play books. Play book number one is our weekly plan. Play book number two is our long-term goal setting.

We want to be goal setters to maximize our time, resources and money making capability. In other words, if you don't know where you are going you will be roaming endlessly. In a word...unproductive.

Weekly sales planning is like the engine that keeps our long-term planning focused and on target. In weekly planning, we are looking to improve the number and quality of sales prospecting calls. We want to put a number up on the board and say "I pledge to make X number of calls every day to reach my weekly goal of Y. I pledge to _____." Make it happen and the outcome will be a great big juicy commission payout.

Another way to look at weekly planning is to commit to selling quantities of products or dollar volumes. This could also involve generating excitement with new customers by focusing calls on newly launched products.

If your territory is in wide geographical area, take the time to carefully map out and plan your calls. A little upfront planning to calculate the drive time to new customers avoids unnecessary rerouting. It's just plain smart. This maximizes every sales prospecting dollar including your time, fuel, parking, etc. and reduces cash burn.

Finally, in weekly sales planning, try to build in a little stretch to make your commissions more attainable. If you are still fresh at the end of a day and can squeeze in one more cold call, do it. The rewards are remarkable.

Long-term goal setting by its very nature is strategic. It's all about the big picture. Focus on making and exceeding monthly, quarterly and lucrative annual budgets, activating juicy bonuses. Long-term goal setting is strategic because, it has a personal growth aspect to it while building essential business skills. Long-term, our goal could be to attain certifications and designations commanding higher pay bases in our business vertical. From a personal perspective, looping all of this data together we become more confident about making large investment purchases such as automobiles and homes. Enjoy this and live your dreams.

Another important part of superior goal setting in sales prospecting is to have your eyes on long-term conversion sales. These tend to be big budget accounts and by their very nature take months, quarters and even years to close. Always have a specific group of long-term conversion accounts in your strategic planning. If you land a long-term conversion account, the wealth generating benefits are a bonanza. In many cases these bonanza accounts grow for years and years to come.

What I'm about to suggest may sound quirky, but, I am always on the lookout for non-conventional revenue on the horizon. We might be approaching an account category so far off our radar that if we land it, it becomes pure topline growth. Look for new product categories you can sell into which might seem unconventional at first but educational and accretive by their very nature.

For example, I do not have a background in accounting or auditing. Yet I have provided sales training in this category. I can see selling more sales training to the legal community as well. Why so? For one simple reason, their business categories are under pressure from freedom of information on the Internet and consumers having access to You Tube teaching aids.

The accounting, legal and professional services groups have recognized the need to learn effective sales prospecting in order to maintain and grow their business.

They do this, even though the very thought of pitching for business is counter intuitive to some of their business profiles and personality styles. Remember, we are in a buyers' market. There are too many sellers and not enough buyers. This makes selling tougher. Buyers are seeking compressed margins and demanding more value added services.

Finally, make your goal setting interesting, fun and achievable. Get creative. Planning takes effort but the rewards are immense.

Here's to reaching your goals. Here's to staying brave and hungry as you march toward sales prospecting victory.

Tips:

1. Use your smart phone to plan calls. Place call information in your Microsoft Outlook Tasks or whichever App you decide to use. Keying in this information as you plan your week and yearly goals ensures you capture ideas and plans as they pop into your mind.

2. Use a large white board in your office. I'm a whiteboard fan and constantly post my short and long-term planning up where I can quickly see and reference items on my action list.

Patrick Tinney

EXERCISE 5 — PLANNING

A. Planning Week

What are your top five ranked goals for next week? Attach a dollar value to `each.

1. _____

_____

2. _____

_____

3. _____

_____

4. _____

_____

5. _____

_____

B. Planning Year

What are your top five ranked goals for the year? Attach a dollar value to each.

1. _____

_____

2. _____

_____

3. _____

_____

4. _____

_____

5. _____

_____

15

CASH IS KING...THE BUYERS' MARKET

"Cash is King".   If you weren't familiar with this phrase, you are now.

During any national or international economic upheaval, it will change the way we all buy and sell. Lenders are skittish. Budgets are scrutinized for efficiencies. Uncertainty will be upon us. Organizations and individuals with cash are in a position to call the shots for a period of time.

For buyers of a variety of products and services this means you have a much wider assortment of buying strategies at your disposal. You are in the enviable position to say no to as many offers as you choose because sellers are lining up to see you.

Buyers, your IQ will appear to have risen remarkably because, sellers will be listening to and dissecting every word you say looking for signs of a *maybe* or a *yes*.

Buyers, this is your time. You can compress time. You can elongate time. You are actually in a good position to bend time and turn time back on pricing.

Sellers, the world just got little more complicated. The marketplace will be taking more time to make decisions about your needs. If your offerings are not absolutely unique and compelling, you will be pressed to show substantially more value than in the past, just to maintain market share. This will require you to be the best sales prospectors in your business category or face declining profit.

Sales prospecting strategies that worked last week may not be relevant this week. Relationships with buyers will change because the market is now wired differently. Even those sellers, who are market leaders with great value propositions and dominant points of difference, will be doing their utmost to lock up as much available revenue from buyers as possible. Why? Because "Cash is King".

Once a dominant seller has secured enough market share and revenue to keep their bankers and shareholders at bay, these sellers will become comfortable projecting forward. Only at this time will they be in a position to sell tougher proposals.

For those of us in business who are not selling a monopoly, we can only "walk away" from a piece of business if it is damaging to us or if we have an equal or better opportunity elsewhere. Dominant sellers locking up base revenue with smart long-term sales proposals will have more confidence to manage future peripheral or pedestrian deals.

In some cases, there may be sellers who are in positions where they may actually be forced to buy business. It sounds odd, but it's true.

Now, because "Cash is King" buyers will feel strong enough to start contacting sellers and asking them, *"Will you take this offer?"* A buyers' market is wired differently and transactional roles may actually be reversed. Sales prospecting skills will truly be tested.

In this environment sellers will have to:

1. Truly understand the customer buying process.
2. Have better customer reconnaissance than competitors.
3. Understand our SWOT (strengths, weaknesses, opportunities, and threats) including competitors and new customers (Lesson 27).
4. Make objectives clear and ranked for importance.
5. Have deep empathy for new prospective customers.
6. Cost model propositions, so as sales proposals are presented with potential agreements, they support our objectives.
7. Be flexible with new customers and show unusual elasticity.

8. Make proposals relevant to buyers. Buyers with cash seek "unique propositions".
9. Know their operations so deeply, they can say "yes" confidently.
10. Be brave. Build smart/wise proposals.

Remember "Cash is King".

Patrick Tinney

PART 2
EXPLORATION &
PLANNING

Patrick Tinney

16

PROFIT THROUGH DISCIPLINED LISTENING

In big budget sales prospecting calls, we must train ourselves to become professional listeners or risk losing out on millions of dollars in sales, savings, or future opportunities.

By nature, most of us are not great listeners. Many sales professionals distract easily. Technology, including smart phones, and other omnipresent hand-held devices, exacerbate our inability to concentrate. I once had a boss who had a television blaring in his office quite often and confessed to having the attention span of a gnat.

The difference between intelligent sales prospecting and other business functions is that you really only get one shot at getting it right. In other words, when you have completed a sale, the last thing you want to do is to re-open the sale. This risks losing what you have gained in the first pass.

To improve your listening skills in big sales prospecting engagements, I recommend:

1.   **Plan meeting objectives** - Do not enter into a big game, sales prospecting call, hoping to think on your feet or depend on your ability as a counter puncher. If

you have well-planned meeting objectives for this sales call, you will have already thought through your strengths, weakness, opportunities, and threats as well as those of your potential customer. This information is helpful in creating your sales tactics and strategy. It will lead to a line of persuasive thinking and questioning designed to draw the other side closer to your objectives. It also helps us to listen for certain pieces of information to verify or discount your knowledge base and strategy.

2.   **Rank high value questions** - In sales prospecting, high value questions are money questions. These questions begin with who, why, where, when, what, how or which. They encourage descriptive answers. I call them money questions, because, I want to rank questions in terms of importance to this important sales call. The questions with the greatest importance to sales prospecting generally have the highest correlation to the revenue/budget. For example, "Who in your organization will benefit most from our proposal?" Listening carefully to the answers to this money question allows our side to ask even deeper questions. It also opens up even greater chances for deeper listening, if we can discipline ourselves to remain silent while the other side responds.

3.   **No unnecessary technology** - If you are going to engage a client and can do so without the use of a smart phone, turn it off. How can you listen if you are glancing at a smart phone while your prospective customer is answering money questions?   Don't let technology cost you a profitable opportunity. Remember, if your prospective customer slips and gives you a sensitive piece of information, it is doubtful they will repeat it.

4.   **Stay in the present** - Focus your thought process. Do not allow your mind to drift backward and forward too much when you are listening to the other side answering money questions. By keeping your mind anchored in the precious present, you will hear more. You will notice more of their body language. This will help you make better decisions about their motives and intentions.

5.   **Using a note taker** - I cannot tell you how advantageous it is to have a note taker in a big game sales prospecting call. This creates an opportunity for one person to ask high value questions and listen. The note taker is totally focused on your potential customer's response. It allows the person asking the questions to have a great impact on the speed and tempo of the call. It may mean your side will get more of your money questions answered. The note taker focuses all his/her energy on capturing the maximum amount of information for later review.

6.   **Practice** - It's tough to listen, when you have great ideas or quick fixes for problems competing for dominance in your mind. Silence is golden in big game

sales prospecting calls. This is particularly powerful after you've asked the high value, money question with the potential to be the tipping point in confirming a product test or a sale.

If you are not a great listener, admit it to yourself and practice more. Disciplined listening does lead to greater big game sales prospecting profits.

17

HIGH VALUE PROSPECTING QUESTIONS

Curiosity in sales prospecting makes money. It's that simple.

The way we channel our sales prospecting curiosity is to ask high value questions. High value questions are those that cannot be answered with a "yes" or a "no".

Examples of high value questions on sales prospecting training are:

1. When and why did you introduce sales prospecting training to your team?
2. What was the big difference in your team after sales prospecting training?
3. What aspect of sales prospecting training will be the most valuable to you and your company?
4. Who on your team needs sales prospecting training?
5. How much new revenue is your company hoping to capture with sales prospecting training?

The person who curiously enquired using the above high value questions would certainly have gained a lot of information on:

1. Timing
2. Corporate culture

3. Response expectations
4. Goals
5. Personnel
6. Budget information

High value questions sometimes called "open-ended" questions are essential to collecting the kind of information we need from prospective buyers. This helps us avoid making assumptions and costly mistakes in sales prospecting.

At my sales training company, Centroid Training, we refer to these "open ended" questions as "armor piercing" questions or "money" questions. The better we are at asking great sales prospecting questions, the more money we will make.

Contextually, if sales prospecting were a military exercise, can you imagine leading a team on to the battlefield without having asked piercing reconnaissance questions regarding the opposing side? Not likely.

An astute sales prospector will have a list of high value questions in her pocket before she enters every client engagement. These questions will be ranked by importance of revenue or objectives.

If the high value questions are delivered in a non-threatening manner, as the other side starts to answer, four important things should happen:

1. The person on our team asking the questions should then assume the role of interviewer. An interviewer's role is to gently encourage the prospective customer to continue with their line of response so that the interviewer can ask deeper questions.
2. If our side is on a four-legged call with the potential new client, the person not asking questions is dedicated to taking detailed notes.
3. After the meeting, these notes are dissected and matched with our ranked list of high value questions and objectives.
4. Finally, a new set of high value questions is created for the next meeting to gain trust and to grow a new client relationship.

The outcome of the meeting may not be as important as the information gathered through well-conceived high value questions.

High value questions in sales prospecting – invaluable.

EXERCISE 6 — HIGH VALUE QUESTIONS

High value questions begin with the words, Why, What, How, When, Which and Where. These questions are designed to extract descriptive answers from prospective customers. These questions cannot be answered with a "yes" or "no". You can also create compound high value questions as shown below.

1. *When and why did you introduce sales prospecting training to your team?*
2. *What was the big difference in your team after sales prospecting training?*
3. *What aspect of sales prospecting training will be the most valuable to you and your company?*
4. *Who on your team needs sales prospecting training?*
5. *How much new revenue is your company hoping to capture with sales prospecting training?*

Keep in mind the above five high value sales prospecting questions as you begin to write your own high value questions. Design your high value questions to fit into your sales prospecting world. Work and re-work your questions until you believe they will result in the greatest insight and response from your prospective customer.

1. _____
   _____
2. _____
   _____
3. _____
   _____
4. _____
   _____
5. _____
   _____
6. _____
   _____

18

TRUE GENIUS IN RECONNAISSANCE

Sir Winston Churchill was one of the finest communicators and influential strategists in modern history.

What Sir Churchill clearly understood and made great strides to improve, was knowledge about all the influential political entities around him. He wanted to understand the strength and reliability of his Second World War allies such as France, Canada, USA, et al. More importantly, he had to gather "reconnaissance" (recon) on his enemies and potential invaders of the United Kingdom.

Recon in sales prospecting has just as vital a role.

Owing to time compression, budgetary pressures and anxiety, too often potential business partners will pull chairs up to a boardroom table, without enough recon on the other side. Not only does this affect your planning, it can also have an impact on your team's confidence, especially, in claiming value, if you have spoken too soon before understanding your potential client's true needs and motives.

The reason we try to uncover large amounts of information in "recon" is to improve the chances of collaborating with a prospective new customer. By encouraging collaboration, the other side will not "run the table with momentum". It means our buyer partner will not push us back on our heels, forcing us to catch up on business intelligence.

There is limitless information we can gather on our new business partners however, recon genius can be found in the following five topics:

1.   **Shared business economics** - Knowing the economic futures and pressure points of our business compared to that of our future business partner will reveal potential strengths or weaknesses.

2.   **New business issues or opportunities** - Understanding new business issues or opportunities for new prospective partners will help us frame our objectives. It will also help us focus on business categories we will want to table during sales engagements. Understanding our partner's objectives will also give us a clearer sense of how far apart we are on key issues. Topics may include new product introductions, new location launches, expansion and planning.

3.   **Points of difference (POD) for both** - Having a clear understanding of our and a new customer's POD will give us the confidence to state our rationale for our costs and pricing. POD also speaks to uniqueness, scarcity, and demand for our product.

4.   **Cost offsets for both** - Arriving at any new customer engagement, understanding in ranked order what you can afford to offer the other side without crippling your own business objectives is paramount. Cost offsets do not necessarily mean money. Cost offsets could be access to technology, relaxed timelines for delivery/warehousing of product, or for payment schedules. It could also mean, access to new services your company is about to offer. Services that the rest of the market has not yet seen but could help your potential buyer partner improve his/her market position. Understanding cost offsets is creatively using what you have already developed at little cost or, absorbed as a cost so reasonably you can now pass it along as a relationship builder. Don't always start with money.

5.   **Profile of buyers** - Often, in new large business engagements, we do a lot of ground work and preparation with one business contact only to find out that a different person will be the lead buyer for our partners at the boardroom table. If this happens, make sure you find out all you can about the new person's ethics, reputation, likes, dislikes, values, and affiliations. All of this information will help you build a profile on this person and improve your ability to soften the impact of the new buyer for their team.

Finally, work at incorporating "true genius" into your new business engagements with crafty recon. Remember Sir Winston Churchill and how he shaped his surroundings by having the capacity for evaluation of uncertain, hazardous, and conflicting information.

19

THE NEED FOR CUSTOMER NAVIGATORS

For as long as I have been a sales prospector, there has been a tug of war between those who want to help us and those who want to thwart our progress. This just happens when we are prospecting larger pieces of business. If we work hard and are fortunate, the person who actually makes the buying decision is the one to pick up their phone. If we can impress this individual with our elevator speech, we may even get an audience with him or her. Alternatively, we may be referred to one of their colleagues who will filter all of the data and information contained in our proposal before presenting it back up to the ultimate decision maker.

In a perfect world, the very person we want to speak to, answers our cold call, meets with us and we get a deal done. All too often, life is not that easy and it certainly is not perfect. This is especially true for businesses engaging new suppliers. Ultimately we end up in one of two camps when we first reach out to our target accounts. Camp number one is where we hit a home run in our first meeting and they become our "navigator". Camp number two is a tougher road and we run into what I call a "stopper". Navigators help us. Stoppers block entry into their business world. Let's take a closer look at the differences between navigators and stoppers. Let's try to understand how to manage from either sales prospecting position.

1.   **Navigators** - A navigator is an amazing partner to have in any customer environment. They are especially important, when we as sales prospectors are trying to learn about their company and how our products and services fit into the overall expenditure landscape. Navigators are characterized by their helping and problem solving attitude toward us. Navigators gently guide us through their important company culture and management architecture. A navigator is able to rank internal company issues and hot buttons. For us, this information is the difference between success and failure. Advanced knowledge of pain points and aspirations, within a prospective customer organization, is the basis on which we can build a compelling case. Advanced knowledge is critical to help us build a storyline to have this company try our product or service. As a sales prospector, we are looking for an opening to have our product work in the customer's environment, in a live profit generation scenario for them. The key to developing a navigator is to assure them that we are looking at their company as a long-term partner. We want to foster a relationship where we as sales professionals can show value in the present, as well as the future. Finally, I believe we have to assure the navigator that we are not just there to interview them and sell them stuff. Our job is to share our newest and neatest market changing ideas, where input from their side suddenly broadens into a collaboration of ideas.

2.   **Stoppers** - A stopper can be anyone at any level in a prospective customer's organization. They feel it is their job to stifle and rebuff our advances. Stoppers are out to protect turf for a variety of reasons. Believe it or not, you can actually have a stopper masquerading as a navigator to slow information flow to us. They try to wear us out in hopes that we will just give up trying to do business with them. Why, you ask? Stoppers have often been known to have high self interest in who receives a piece of business. It may have to do with how the stopper benefits from the current supplier. Another scenario is where the stopper can actually be grinding old axes. They are not going to give up on their grudge against us until something dramatic happens on their end. In my newspaper sales days, I was pitching advertising space to one of Canada's big box stores. As hard as I tried with great proposals and great research, I could not move this account. It took a fair amount of digging but I later found out that the newspaper in question had reported on some unusual local activity with this account causing a break in relations. Ouch. No wonder I had a stopper. The news I didn't know was that the home office for

Patrick Tinney

this retailer was not happy with the performance from this market. My navigator from the customer's home office called me over a year later and whispered into the phone. *"Please dust off your proposal and bring it in now. There has been a personnel change within our organization in the market you have been pitching to us."*

There are a few important lessons to take away from this. Work on building navigators wherever you go. Even if they don't work out immediately, they will understand you are trying to build a bridge respectfully. Secondly, stoppers can suddenly become navigators if economic, management or budgetary circumstances change within the customer's world. Finally, navigators and stoppers can be found in home office environments, regional and local offices. All of these parties want similar things. It has to do with profit and stable growth.

20

HIDDEN KEYS FOR DOORS TO ELUSIVE SALES PROSPECTS

Prospecting for sales inside large corporations is tremendously rewarding, especially if you are able to penetrate the barriers surrounding the important stake holders. One of the big problems I find is that large corporations have built huge walls and deep moats around themselves. Only the chosen few are granted entry. In other words, large corporations choose suppliers carefully and try to avoid talking to companies they believe do not meet their current or future needs.

Internet search engines have given prospectors valuable insight into the lives and viewpoints of business decision makers. We can view corporation websites and read industry reports where executives have been profiled or quoted. On the rare occasion, corporations and senior executives publish industry white papers to lobby for change and raise their profile with potential new customers.

Social media outlets such as LinkedIn, Twitter and even Facebook have provided yet another entry point for sales prospectors to reach out to executive decision makers. By sending invitations to join our business networks, joining social media groups and other public chat forums, we can create new business relationships.

Patrick Tinney

Question? What if you know that you want to meet a VP Marketing or a SVP Operations at a corporation? The challenge is, their names do not appear on any reports and there is no one who will respond to you with a contact entry point. Worse yet, you run into gatekeepers posing as personal assistants, who are really blockers with high self-interest. What do you do?

Here are a few hidden keys for contacting elusive sales prospects in large corporations.

Accounts Receivable Department - The neat thing about calling an Accounts Receivable Department in any large corporation is that there will almost always be someone there to pick up the phone or call you back quickly. Why? It's because accounts receivable employees are always looking to collect cash from slow paying clients. The other neat thing is accounts receivable employees have a pretty tough job. Therefore, speaking to an outsider who is not trying to dupe them out of money can actually be a pleasant conversation. More importantly, they may well turn out to be your company navigator, if you treat them respectfully. Accounts receivable is often linked to sales. Therefore, they can be a wealth of information about the department or individuals you are attempting to reach. I have often called accounts receivable departments. They are open and generally good people to talk to.

The Research Department - The Research Department in many cases works closely with product development, sales and marketing. So they are connected to a lot of people in the company. A call to them could yield nice results for information on senior executives. Guess what? They too pick up their phones. Just recently, I was trying to get copies of my new book "Unlocking Yes" to a television show in New York City. The books were initially rejected by the station's gatekeepers. Determined to get my book into the right hands, I called their Analytics Expert and he did indeed pick up his phone. After a lively exchange of ideas, he agreed to accept delivery of my books and personally distribute them to the other key anchors of the television show. This was a great win.

The Legal Department - The Legal Department is a great department to call if you want to get someone to call you back. Again, people in the legal department will generally pick up their phones because they are adept at talking to the public without causing any exposure or risk to the company. Secondly, if you say "I want to talk to someone in the legal department" a lot of red lights go off. If the legal department won't talk to you, they will make sure the department you do want to talk to responds. Nobody wants to mess with the legal department.

Branch Offices - In the old days in the newspaper business, our head office customers would regularly end run us by calling our newspapers directly, rather than speaking to our central sales office. Inevitably, these customers gained a ton of information on our central sales office and on the operations of the newspapers. Contacting a local branch office or outlet may garner valuable insights into your prospective new customer.

The President's Office - Calling the President's Office is really a calculated risk. The President is the company's number one salesperson. She/he is the ultimate decision maker. The upside is when you make a positive impression with the President, they will refer you to the correct person along with a personal note. There is nothing better than this. The downside is if you do not impress the President, your pitch has come to an end. As I say, it's a calculated risk.

The corporate world is filled with keys to doors we as sales prospectors need to open. You just have to be brave enough to pick up the phone and not be afraid of failure. Note to self. Stay brave and strong.

21

WHY PROBLEM SOLVERS WIN

Having the mindset of a problem solver always struck me as one of the surest ways to grow new customers. In our current global recessionary environment, being a problem solver is a must. The reason is, large companies are very hesitant to switch suppliers if business is running smoothly. The problem is competition never rests. Technology never rests and, pricing is market dependent.

The very best sales prospectors know, to make their case for a customer to change or add a supplier, they need to identify business implications and leverage points. In many cases, it comes down to a discussion about our company point of difference. This includes how we effectively fill a hole in the customer's operations. Filling holes that could make the customer smarter, faster, better and more profitable will appeal to our prospective client.

Therefore, we are either unearthing a customer's threats and weaknesses (business implications) or we are making a case for our ability to improve the customer's strengths and opportunities (key leverage points).

Having a great understanding of the customer's business category and having an equally profound understanding of how our product offerings improve the customer's world is vital. I am amazed at how the smartest sales problem solvers book an appointment to meet with a new customer and leave the meeting with not one sale but several. Here are several reasons why being a sales problem solver will rapidly move us up the customer's revenue expenditure food chain.

Smart/creative solutions - Customers will pay handsomely for creative solutions to improve their operations and profitability. With the complexity of technology, many businesses are totally reliant on suppliers to keep them up to date and ahead of their competitors. If we can prove to a customer that our creative solution is unique, they will talk to us and perhaps even give us a tracked field test.

Lowest impact - It's a cliché but "time is money". Any excessive downtime with implementation of a new product or service gives new clients sweaty palms. Nonetheless, if we are able to physically demonstrate to the client our product works as promised, we will receive high marks for our efforts. And, receive the much coveted "the proof is in the pudding" test with the client.

Best cost - We now live in a buyers' market. There are far too many sellers and there is simply little time for buyers to examine each new innovation. One thing that does catch a buyer's eye is cost saving. Many customers will tell you that cost is the only thing on their minds. Believe me, quality matters to them as well. There is nothing worse than buying on cost and then having the product fall apart on delivery. The sweet spot is to be both cost effective and have a margin of quality helping senior management in a corporation sleep easy.

Honest - Being straight up with a prospective client is not a weakness. If we de-risk your product, they can factor in waste or modest exposure. As a category manager for the flyer distribution business at a large media company, I had a competitor who boldly explained to customers that if you bought his flyer delivery service you could expect "X" percentage waste. My competitor's waste number was much higher than that of my company. Granted, my competitor's pricing was lower, but they occasionally won business for their perceived candor.

Quick response - Everyone involved in a change in suppliers knows there is a modicum of risk. The risk, however, is always softened by the swiftness of response. Customers don't want to hear that a hiccup with a change in suppliers could take days or weeks to fix. Customers want action. If our company promises action resulting from any volatility in delivery of our product or service, we better deliver. Consequently, if we do deliver as promised, the new suppliers stock rises substantially. The thinking is that problems are always lurking. Quick response is the neutralizer and trust builder.

Best competition - Any time we as sales prospectors beat our competition, we are opening the door to rising up the customer's expenditure food chain. Therefore, a careful examination and understanding of our competitor's offering, quality, pricing and response level is crucial. If we conduct a SWOT (strengths, weaknesses, opportunities and threats) analysis on our competitors we will learn to copy and improve their best ideas. We will also learn to gently expose their weaknesses and threats to customers in a way that makes us look like a concerned supplier and a trusted advisor, rather than a fear monger. (More in Lesson #28)

We have now learned problems are not always negatives in sales prospecting. Problems solved with creativity and gusto is the gateway to long lasting success with new sales prospects.

22

BRAND ALIGNMENT AND ITS INFLUENCES

Brand alignment in the contemporary sense, is the alignment of all communication, cultural, and marketing efforts. This presents a brand as one continuous stream of thought to the consumer. Our brand alignment must address our corporate position in the market, relative to our clients and our selling peers. In sales prospecting brand alignment has the potential to greatly influence our approach to new customers.

Brand alignment for corporate sales/buyer partnerships could mean we have customers, standards of excellence, or aspirations in common. These common elements naturally create an attraction for doing business together. Therefore, prospecting a new business partner whose needs profile fits our own makes for a matching or more-leveled playing field. For example, in the daily newspaper business, one of the closest matches we had from a customer market profile perspective was major department stores. At the time research verified daily newspaper readers were also very much aligned to the major department store customer ideal. This did not mean our sales prospecting proposals were "open net goals". It only meant we both understood we had a lot of compelling common ground.

Patrick Tinney

This alignment can happen anywhere in the business spectrum from the ultra-high end of the business market to the low end of the business market. The cliché *"birds of a feather flock together"* comes to mind.

If direct brand alignment is a benefit to both parties in a new sales/buyer relationship, what does it mean for businesses that are interested in each other but are further up or down the ideal pecking order? In a word, it's a "challenge".

In Toronto, Canada, we are blessed with five daily newspapers. To one degree or another all of these newspapers are very well aligned to specific readers and advertisers. Therefore, they are in a ranked pecking order up or down by advertisers. In this setting, residing in the first or second market preference position with an advertiser is a much sought after sales prospecting position. Residing in the third or fourth market preference positions becomes a sales prospecting conundrum. Those daily newspapers on the perimeter high or low market positions have a huge challenge convincing advertisers that they are simpatico with opposite brand customers and quality requirements.

We have used daily newspapers as an example but, the same conversation about brand alignment in sales prospecting could just as easily be shifted to home appliances, smart phone devices, or packaged goods.

Elements that equalize a lack of brand alignment in sales prospecting include the following:

Creativity - Customers buy creative ideas over "stuff" any day of the week. Our company may be in the number three pecking position but, if we have creative solutions for a customer to attract new markets and add value; this is a great brand alignment equalizer.

Innovation - This is where we take unique brand parts and do something really neat to help our customer be smarter, faster or better. If we can show a customer how to make money, we are bound to get a longer client engagement. Innovation is an equalizer.

Quality - Having access to various iterations of our product in various sizes, styles, positions, formats or color is an attention-grabber. If our company has the ability and agility to modify quality of a product to suit a budget or a market place, we are showing great flexibility. Guess what? We have another brand alignment equalizer.

Technology - Lots of customers love to be on the cutting edge of technology to give them an advantage in the market over their competitors. Technology may be something our company owns outright. It could be a new use of the Internet. It could be as simple as a new use for a symbol. Just think, a few years ago, hardly anyone had heard of a *"Quick Response Code"*. For those who first adopted QR Codes, they had a period of stylish, nerdy, uniqueness so sought after in today's fickle consumer and business market.

Time - Finding or saving time has the potential to give customers a strategic advantage over competitors and quite possibly save them money in the process. This is another great brand alignment equalizer.

Price - We've purposely saved price until last because, anyone can lower price without thinking about the long-term ramifications this causes their brand. These ramifications could affect the very alignment they are seeking with a potentially important customer.

If we are lowering price for a well-placed strategy - bravo! If we are lowering price to maintain market share and keep feeding the troops – noble. The question remains, what is our exit plan? If we are buying business to make it to the next round of payments, then I say, over to you.

When our company is trying to solve the problem of brand alignment in sales prospecting, make sure our team does a customer needs assessment first. Think creativity, innovation, quality, technology, and timing to level the playing field. Leave price last.

23

SPEAK THE CUSTOMER'S LANGUAGE FOR GREATER SUCCESS

As a boy and a young man, I had the benefit of working in many retail environments. I really liked all of the activity associated with retail. I just loved engaging new customers and listening to the cash register ring. When I went on to college, I chose a full time Retail Advertising Program as my course of study. Once again, I was bathing in the retail world as it related to advertising and marketing. I graduated college and took a job in Western Canada working on a retail account list at a community newspaper. I quickly moved from newspaper to newspaper growing my retail advertising skills and had great success in this retail channel.

At age 24, I landed a job at Canada's largest daily newspaper, The Toronto Star. I worked my way into a busy retail territory, working with large retail accounts such as Toys R Us, FW Woolworth and others. Next, I moved on to Canada's largest daily newspaper chain, The Southam Newspapers Group. You guessed it…in the retail department. I initially reported to a brilliant Vice President and Retail Titan named Stan Shortt.

Stan recognized my raw talent for selling to retail, but, quickly realized I had a strength we needed to bolster, if I wanted to really be accepted by many of North America's largest retailers. My new accounts included major department stores, junior department stores and big box retailers. With Stan's immense retail knowledge base and his great patience, he immersed me in the detailed language of retail.

Don't roll your eyes. Believe me, retail is a language and it takes years to learn if you want to communicate as an insider and an equal with the juggernauts of this industry. For example, under Mr. Shortt's tutelage, I no longer used the term "merchandise selection". I replaced this phrase with "assortment of merchandise" and "breadth and depth of merchandise". I could go on. I had to learn and replace a lot of my earlier language with retail. You see, speaking newspaper didn't matter to my new customer base. It was all about speaking retail. This allowed me to be much more creative with ideas and incentive plans I would produce and present to the customer. I was given much more accord with these retail giants. I was also warmly accepted among my newspaper peers and retail counter parts. I was finally a retail specialist working in the newspaper business.

I have many fond memories working with my retail colleagues. I still count several as close friends. One of the neatest experiences I had involved a phone call from the media manager of Walmart. I was invited to represent the newspaper industry. It was an invitation to present my businesses best and most creative ideas to Walmart's entire Canadian marketing team comprised of 40+ marketing executives. It was a marvelous opportunity.

I quarterbacked a team of four crack account managers and sales managers. We pulled together an eye popping presentation based on Walmart's needs. Weeks later our newspaper team presented Walmart with a crisp, on the edge of your seat, 40 minute presentation. We got wide applause and great personal praise from the Walmart team as our team wrapped up and left their building.

Certainly if Stan Shortt, former Vice President with two of Canada's major department stores had not taught me how to speak fluent retail, I question whether the Walmart experience, in their inner sanctum, ever would have happened. If I had not been able to speak the language of the largest retailer in the world, I would have been just another newspaper guy, talking about newspaper stuff.

So, my sales friends and colleagues learn to speak your customer's language and your sales prospecting success will be much greater than you ever could have imagined. You will earn respect from your prospective customers. More importantly, your awareness of their world will open new customer relationships and much coveted trust. Based on your ability to acclimate to your customer's world, speaking in their language, you will become a "go to professional" who speaks like an insider.

24

PRODUCT KNOWLEDGE BUILDS CONFIDENCE

I am a great believer that customers buy sales professionals first, products second and national brands third. Why that particular order you ask? I believe it comes down to the confidence that the sales professional exhibits in explaining the vast array of options accompanied with buying a product or product eco system.

Great salespeople are like navigators. If they are honest and confident they can effectively explain the incredible benefits of their products while intelligently exposing any potential risk to the potential buyer. This product knowledge delivered by a product expert allows customers to sleep easy after making a major purchase. This product knowledge removes buyer's remorse even if the customer has purchased a superior product at a premium price.

Superior sales professionals deliver profound knowledge so clearly new customers are confident in buying from this product expert over and over again. It also gives customers the confidence to recommend this sales professional to their closest business colleagues.

As a newspaper flyer distribution manager and production specialist, I referred to the brightest of my flyer colleagues as "wizards". Wizards are knowledgeable, reliable and creative navigators. They guide new customers through complicated sales processes.

As sales professionals we have to be able to explain, in simple language, the ins and outs of purchasing our products and services. Let's review a few product knowledge subjects that, when explained concisely, remove any doubt that we are the only salesperson the customer will want to deal with going forward.

1.   **Product innovations** - Having the ability to explain amazing product innovation that will improve the customer's world is a great talent. Customer's love to feel that they are on the leading edge of tomorrow's next great wave. It's almost as if the salesperson is sharing a secret. A secret the customer can go away with and immediately look for ways to further embed this innovation into their lives so they live smarter, faster and better.

2.   **Demonstrations** - Being able to pull your product apart and put it back together effortlessly makes the customer feel as if they also will be able to do it too with a little practice. If we sales professionals fumble through a product demonstration can you imagine what the customer is thinking?   Believe it or not, I had a research provider show up for a sales meeting unprepared to demonstrate and explain his research reports. He arrived at my office without a notebook and pen. I was stunned and quite frankly annoyed that this person was wasting my time and money. In my view, he was not prepared to do business let alone service business.

3.   **Research presentation** - Great research presenters are magical to observe. They embody the best of analytical skills, presentation skills and showmanship. If you are never going to be a great research presenter make sure you take your research professional with you on important prospective customer calls. This is not considered a weakness. It is smart business.

4.   **Creative ideas** - Important prospective customers expect our best ideas. New customers want to be shown how they can grow their business profitability by using our product. Prospective customers want to feel like they are getting a leg up on their competitors if they buy our product idea. Our best ideas when executed flawlessly make the purchaser look like a genius in front of their peers and superiors.

5.   **Specifications/deadlines** - You might think details such as specifications and deadlines are the boring stuff that gets turned over to some production person to figure out at her own peril. Not so. By properly explaining specifications and

deadlines around purchasing our products and services, with great ease, sales professionals are displaying their wizardry. They are also de-risking the sale to an important new customer. Steve Cosic, former Director of Media Procurement for The Hudson's Bay Company used to say time and again "the devil is in the details".

6.   **Delivery/execution** - Having the ability to align the customer's expectations for delivery and execution of our products and services has a calming effect on customers. Life is not perfect. At times delivering product is not perfect. Customers get this. Notwithstanding, no customer wants to be negatively surprised because we were not knowledgeable enough to walk him/her through this phase of the sale. Be smart. De-risk the sales process by aligning expectations and explain back up plans should anything not function perfectly on delivery. Customer's rely on and expect this level of product knowledge and service.

7.   **Follow-up** - Assuring a prospective customer that all deliveries of large purchases comes with follow up, demonstrates that we are not "trunk slammers" who take customers money and disappear. It shows that we have integrity and that this new customer will have the best possible experience with our product. Letting a customer know you personally care is the height of sales professionalism. This legitimizes our great product knowledge and lets prospective customers know that we will be there to assist and make good on our product promises no matter what the circumstance.

Patrick Tinney

25

CUSTOMER PLANNING IS CRITICAL

Accomplished sales prospectors know the best way to understand the breadth of budget expenditure possibilities with a new customer is to understand how the customer's quarterly and annual expenditure planning works. It is critical to understand when in the calendar year this planning takes place. Bringing key proposals to the prospective customer six to twelve weeks in advance, will position us for greater success. This is especially important if you plan to dislodge a long time vendor competitor.

In some cases, planning by product line may happen separately within the broader annual financial planning process. We want to have an idea of when this is happening for exactly the same reasons.

In order to focus the correct amount of time, energy and resources, we also want to know where this potential account is ranked in our annual targets. We also want to know what impact this account will have on our revenue targets, should we succeed in opening discussions with this account for a test or sale.

If we have not previously done business together, it always helps to know where our company sits on the prospective customer's radar. If we are developing new systems, products or services, this could move us up on their "investigate screen".

The following information should be taken into consideration when presenting pricing in opening proposals to a new customer.

1.   **Planning location** - Knowing where our prospective client does its planning is important. This is especially important if our prospective client has a national or a global presence. Often global companies with senior executive teams are located in several different countries. Knowing where their head office is located does not guarantee that the buyer planning is done in that office. Each office may be responsible for its own planning and revenue targets. Having this information upfront saves time and resources.

2.   **Duration of planning** - Generally, the smaller the prospective company, the shorter the planning should be. The problem is we cannot count on this rule of thumb. It is best to ask some questions around planning duration, so we can calibrate our expectations for any approvals that might take place and their effect on our business.

3.   **Planning participants** - Whether we are talking about small businesses or large corporations there is someone who coordinates planning funnels. This can be a small team or a committee who is aggregating budgets and expenditure requirements. This is done so the overall budget matches the strategic planning for the company. Therefore, for our product line, identify who holds accountability for our vertical business budget and if these buying decisions are delegated to someone other than the budget owner.

4.   **Outside planning participants** - Increasingly, small and large businesses are seeking advice from outside partners or third party suppliers. This trend can be both positive and negative. Positive, if the third party supplier does so in a low self-interest manner. Negative, if outside parties are trying to exercise influence with the home company by making exaggerated predictions about market potential and their influence on this potential. Some large corporations in the advertising business, for instance, will separate the media buying from the media planning. This creates a focus on excellence for all parties involved.

5.   **Influencers** - We must keep our eyes and ears open for influencers with prospective customers. Corporations with family groups who own different

Patrick Tinney

portions of the business are an excellent example of how influence can come into play. Again, don't rule out third party influencers who sell products and services such as consumer research, to sway budgeting decisions.

6.   **Budget size** - The reason we want to know budget size relative to our product offering, is that we want the right sized proposal prepared for the right sized opportunity. Size matters in this case.

7.   **Vendor review process** - Many businesses are now employing procurement specialists within their firms, in order to separate buyers from sellers and remove relationship factors. The focus then becomes largely a quality/price discussion. Another approach is the use of brokerage houses and procurement third party agents to carry out high volume buying. This creates one more layer of complexity and generally a longer buying decision process.

8.   **Approval process** - Understanding buying approval processes is vital. The group doing all of the gathering and projections of forward planning for a company may only be a percentage of the approval process. Companies with deep management layers, tend to have very heavy senior management approval processes, destined to stretch out buying decisions. Flatter company structures are generally a little quicker to act. Remember, adverse competitive or economic environments can slow down any decision making process at any time.

9.   **Preferred vendors** - If a company has a preferred vendor program, I want to know about it. This generally means, that the company we are prospecting takes a longer range view of vendors and the true value they bring to the table. Price, regardless of our offering, will be a factor. Price gets more illuminated as buying volumes come into play.

I must underscore the importance of having a full picture of your prospective customer's planning. Every dollar we misplace with proposals and creative ideas delivered to the wrong person, at the wrong time, is money borrowed, lent and even lost. Note to self. Dig deep on customer planning and approval processes.

26

TRACK COMPETITOR PRICING

Pricing is the elephant in the room with sales prospecting. It is especially so when we present our pricing to a prospective customer and they start to compare what we offer versus our competitors.

Prospecting for sales is much easier in a sellers' market, where there are too many buyers and not enough sellers. It is a supply game and we have product to pump into a demand hungry market place. As a seller we enjoy the option of bending toward the customer with pricing. Conversely, we can hold firm with pricing, betting the customer will come back to us. There is always the potential of our products being sold out in a short window of time, owing to market demand which makes indecision an unsafe bet for the customer. Ah…those were the days.

Since the financial market meltdown of 2008 there has been a problem with large and small corporations growing their topline sales. We have had a global slowdown in demand. Buyers have become a lot more selective about what they buy, when they buy and how they buy. This tightening of buying conditions has caused a seller conundrum. Businesses the world over have been reviewing their entire business operations to cut the fat. They have been doing this to free up more elasticity in pricing while still showing profitable results on their balance sheets.

There still remains a problem however. Topline sales are becoming tougher to maintain and growth profile accounts are becoming harder to find. As a result, sales prospecting has become that much more important.

Our competitors are being forced to make tough choices because their customers are demanding better pricing and value. This puts pressure on the entire stream of the product category in which we participate. In choppy markets conditions such as I have described, it is imperative to track competitor pricing. This pricing collection helps us make more intelligent decisions about our own pricing. It also affects our product offerings especially around the elasticity of quality and time. Time and quality requirements are important to our prospective customers and our profitability. In the arena of competitor pricing, collect competitor pricing in as many competitor pricing scenarios as possible. Here are some potential sources.

1.   **Rate cards** - Unless your company is in a fixed cost business category, rate cards in savvy buyer's eyes are the beginning of a discussion. You will be tested to justify your pricing. Unless, your product or service has a very compelling point of difference, your customers will be looking at several suppliers in your business vertical. So, collect competitor rate cards.

2.   **Current pricing** - In a tight buyers' market current pricing can change as commodity input costs change or as new cost cutting synergies can be found. Hidden added value by your competitors can also mask real net/net pricing. Tracking this is highly valuable.

3.   **Thresholds** - Not all pricing thresholds are created equally. In many cases lower frequency customers pay a premium price while heavy usage customers can actually overwhelm many cost models. This is why, as alert business people, we have to keep prospecting for new customers so we can continually spread the risk of price compression, owing to having too many large account customers.

4.   **Corner cases** - While I did not condone it as a regular practice in my corporate selling days, it was necessary to take a look at "must have" bell weather customers. Under the right conditions a price lowering strategy might be justified to undermine a competitor. Buying a customer out from under a competitor in a particular market without causing nation-wide price contagion can be an effective strategy. These are corner cases and you can bet your competitors have them too.

5.   **Test rates** - As a regular practice, test rates are prickly beasts. You want the customer to try your product live in the field. You don't want them to believe

that you can deliver this lower introductory pricing without justifiable volume expenditures from the customer. Your competitors might also have test rates. If you analyze them closely there is valuable information to be had in understanding your competitor's profitability and overall corporate health.

6.   **Dollar volume** - I really detest dollar volume rates. They are profit negative in most businesses. Dollar volume pricing allows one buying agent to act as a central buying and billing source for many potential clients. This creates false volume levels detrimental to your business. It also creates a scenario where the central buyer agent wields power beyond his/her mandate. As a participant in a pricing committee for my former employer, our group reviewed pricing models from across the world in our business category. Dollar volume contracts were by far, the most profit destructive models we analyzed. If your competitors are using dollar volume contracts, there is good reason to believe they are looking for short term gains and heading for long-term pain.

Pricing is an expression of value. Value is crystalized in the eye of the buyer. When you start to eye some of your competitors business, make sure you do your homework on the profitability of the business. Confirm the true value your competitor is offering for any customer pricing. Trust your prospective customers, but verify their price claims, especially, when it involves matching or beating one of your direct competitors on price.

27

POWER SWOT BEFORE MAJOR PROSPECTING

If we want to go fishing for "whale-sized" accounts, a very powerful exercise prior to any major sales prospecting engagement is a SWOT (strengths, weaknesses, opportunities, and threats) analysis of our business relative to a potential sale. Professional sales prospectors go much further with this exercise and SWOT their competitors and their potential new buyer partner.

Why SWOT? The answer is why wouldn't you? This analysis, if performed honestly, helps us bring greater light to our position with our potential buying partner. It also helps you formulate strategy, plans, and tactics that we will want to bring to a sales proposal for the new client meeting.

The SWOT exercise sounds pretty academic, but it's surely the one that gives salespeople the greatest uneasiness. While training a very mature sales force, I was amazed that SWOT analysis was an "AHA Moment" for them.

It can be difficult for us to be objective, especially when facing a potentially difficult business proposal presentation. Most of us have a fairly easy time discussing our strengths and opportunities, because as business people, we live in the present and future where we are strong and robust. We sell best when we project from a position of strength.

Conversely, in corporate life, it's not very popular to speak excessively about weaknesses and threats. After all, aren't we professionals at turning customer objections into sales? Can't we just figure problems out and come up with sensible solutions?

By honestly detailing weakness and threats, we are opening the door to intelligent discussion about exposure to negative business implications. This can actually help us raise our game, fix holes in our defense and better prepare us to hear customer objections. By showing customer empathy, it allows us to honestly say, *"We, too, are concerned about this issue, and this is what we are doing to address this weakness."* Honesty has the potential to hasten strategic solutions and possibly thwart competitors with our innovative ideas.

Back to the positive. By studiously adding up our strengths and opportunities, we can clearly see key leverage points used to persuade our potential buying partners to move closer to our sales prospecting objectives. After all, everyone wants to participate with a winner, especially, when both sides experience financial and emotional fulfillment.

What about a SWOT analysis on our closest competitors? Smart move. My lifetime in business has taught me there are simply no safe accounts, no safe markets, and no safe deals. Our competitors are constantly changing the playing field with new innovations, new product launches, new acquisitions, and new partnerships.

For example, in recent years suppliers have moved their own people into customers' head offices to become a seamless, influential part of the customer's team. The rub is that these suppliers are doing this by assuming the cost of equipment and personnel to take pressure off diminishing resources on the customer's side. The upside is that these suppliers are solidifying long-term deals with this strategy.

Finally, what about a SWOT analysis of our potential buying partner? Doubly smart move. This focuses us on understanding their world with greater intensity and empathy. If they are trying to build revenue or market share that we can positively affect through our innovation – what a gift of knowledge this is heading into a large sales proposal presentation.

On the other hand, by understanding their weaknesses and threats, we can ask some pretty well-placed questions about what is keeping our potential buyer partner up at night. Again, all of this information just strengthens our ability to be more decisive with our sales prospecting strategy.

By trying to see ourselves through our customer's eyes, we are really exposing our side to the deepest truth one can hope to uncover prior to a proposal presentation. What if we are in love with our "point of difference" in the market, but our customer could really care less and actually does not agree with our wonderful assessment of us? Yikes!

The neat thing about all of the above analysis is that if time is compressed, we can actually write a mini SWOT on the back of a napkin sitting in a waiting room heading into a proposal presentation meeting. This advanced sales prospecting methodology is how sales professionals scratch out those precious, extra points while closing important sales.

So here's the question: How good and dedicated is your team at SWOT analysis, heading into major sales proposal presentations? If the answer is "not great," I highly recommend you seek out a professional sales facilitator to help your team learn to power SWOT effectively to scratch out those precious, extra points while closing out on big game sales.

28

SWOT <u>COMPETITORS</u> BEFORE PROSPECTING

Preparation for a major sales prospecting presentation involving large budget contracts cuts a wider swath. Not only do you need to have a great proposal in hand with brilliant creative options, you need to be prepared for a feisty battle with competitors who are trying to expand their position with your potential customer.

A thorough SWOT of your competitors' position in your industry, often yields great ideas for your upcoming key customer presentations. By looking at your competitor's strengths/opportunities and weaknesses/threats, you will identify the gaps between your offerings. This will help you gain the upper-hand and grow your share of business with major customers.

To begin, you must gather every piece of available information on your competitors through industry analysis, quarterly stock market reports, business blogs/articles, and of course your competitor's websites. This sounds like a huge undertaking but, with robust search engine capabilities and crafty queries, you'd be surprised what you can gather with a few stealth clicks.

There is no perfect place to start a SWOT analysis, but I prefer to know as much about my competitor's strengths/opportunities, also known as "Key Leverage

Patrick Tinney

Points". They will almost always base their proposals with key leverage points, highlighting their unique product and service offerings in the market place. I want to know these key leverage points before I stand in front of a frosty customer who may use my competitor's offerings as a tool to dampen or diminish my proposal.

Competitors' key leverage points (strengths/opportunities) may include:

1. New product development
2. New technology
3. New markets
4. Strategic alliances
5. Cutting edge research
6. Innovative test results
7. Flexible packaging and delivery
8. And....great pricing

By understanding competitor key leverage point data, you will be able to adjust your proposal to address the above issues in a way that becomes a game-changer for your potential large customer. The customer will no doubt, respect the amount of time you have taken to analyze and anticipate their key needs and thereby reduce the anxiety of supplier changes.

Next, you want to know all about your competitors' weaknesses/threats also known as "Business Implications". By understanding your competitors' daily worries you can strategically weave this intelligence into your proposals to your potential major client and to your advantage.

Notable business implications (weakness/threats) to look for will include:

1. Geographical gaps
2. Technology glitches
3. Misaligned market offerings
4. Quality performance
5. Supply chain bottlenecks
6. Staffing/union problems
7. Senior management stability
8. Storage/delivery reliability and tracking
9. Problem resolution response times....to mention a few

When you are able to effectively bundle a 360 degree analysis of your competitors through a SWOT analysis, you are able to plan for most large customer queries during a sales presentation. Your mission is to respond with quick, crisp competitor alternatives in a live presentation setting. Follow up this action with inspired objection handling/ value statements such as:

"We hear what you are saying."

"We have been monitoring these events in the market."

"We appreciate your interest and concerns."

"Speaking of which, here is a great solution and opportunity we have developed."

"We look forward to sharing it with you and your team of experts for seamless implementation."

"This is why our customers continue to call us first because we develop creative solutions. We anticipate critical needs."

Be smart. Work to capture more than your share of your prospective customer's available expenditures. Power SWOT your competitors' so you can focus more on the customer's needs while producing creative, revenue-winning proposals.

29

SWOT Your <u>Customer</u> Before A Sales Proposal Presentation

Performing a SWOT analysis on a major customer before a business proposal presentation is not only smart, it is a necessity. It is analogous to a surgeon ordering an MRI x-ray of a patient before performing major surgery. If our new customer proposal is critical to our company, the depth of the SWOT analysis should reflect this.

When we combine the customer's strengths and opportunities (key leverage points), we are looking for openings to help the customer drive their business forward propelled by our products and services. This helps us approach the customer with creative ideas helping to crystalize their opportunities that appear out of reach for them. This will further our cause in closing a deal. This allows us to table unique solutions for unique clients that are not as price sensitive.

Let's face it, customers know they have pain points. I believe the scale has tipped too far in many sales categories in driving this dogma home. "We've all been to the business house of horrors". Instead, let's first talk to the customer about great beginnings and great untapped opportunities. Opportunities, only we can provide with our point of difference.

Our customer's key leverage points (strengths/opportunities) may include:

1. New product development
2. New technology or better supplier sourcing
3. New product launches
4. Unique points of difference
5. Unique product or market verticals
6. New markets
7. Strategic purchases causing potential new efficiencies
8. Faster and more flexible packaging and delivery
9. Traditional and 2.0 sales possibilities, plus great pricing

With this preparation, the customer will respect the amount of time we have taken to analyze and anticipate their key needs. This type of positive risk thinking on our part is a "game-changer".

Next, we want to know all about our customer's weaknesses/threats, also known as "business implications". By understanding our customer's daily worries we can strategically weave this intelligence into our proposal, to our advantage.

Notable business implications (weakness/threats) we look for include:

1. Market share erosion
2. Profit erosion
3. Geographical gaps
4. Technology shortcomings
5. Traditional customer competitors
6. Non-traditional customer competitors
7. Over supply positions
8. Recent internal and external sales disruptions
9. Brand instability/erosion

When we are able to effectively bundle a 360 degree analysis of our large customer through a SWOT analysis, we are able to think as if we were walking in their shoes. We want our proposal to be meaningful, constructive, and incremental to their business. If we get the trajectory of our proposal right and presented to key decision makers, it opens up the possibility for a stream of trial closes that sound like this:

Patrick Tinney

a. *"What about our proposal did you like the most?"*
b. *"Who in your organization will benefit from our proposal?"*
c. *"How would you like to begin rolling out our proposal?"*

Winning a large account business deal starts by thinking like an insider. If we can figure out where the customer sees the greatest opportunity for growth or the greatest need for defensive measures, then we are part of their team. Think in terms of the customer's culture and forward strategic planning. If we breathe their rarified air, we will be rewarded for our extra effort.

30

TIME MANAGEMENT IS FOR PROSPECTING WINNERS

For reasons I cannot explain, I have always been acutely aware of time. In the business world, I despised being late for meetings or having my meeting partner wander in a half hour late. Time is truly about money. And if you are late for a meeting, you are spending someone else's money.

In sales prospecting, if you are not keeping tabs on time you will miss opportunities. You will either dawdle or allow yourself to be distracted. Consequently, you will not spend the right amount of time with customers that have money which they are prepared to spend.

I am not advocating that you as a sales prospector be on a stop-watch with important prospective customers. What I am saying is, work smart not hard. Prospect when you know you can access important clients. Do your homework and find out when they are most apt to respond to you or pick up the phone and explore your offerings with you in Q & A.

In order to squeeze the most out of daily sales prospecting and to hit your sales targets earlier consider the following:

Patrick Tinney

1.   **Daily planning** - If you end every day with a carefully constructed sales prospecting plan, then you are set to run the very next day. There is no big thinking because your day is laid out in front of you and all you have to do is keep making calls according to your plan. If you blow through your plan ahead of time and have an extra hour at the end of the day, take advantage of this. It's a gift. Make one more call and close a deal.

2.   **Clear objectives** - By clearly understanding mission objectives you are less likely to get blown off course during the day. Should this happen, have a little chat with yourself and get refocused. Focus is the key to making more successful sales prospecting calls.

3.   **Preparation** - Some salespeople like to wing sales prospecting calls and counter punch with the customer to gain information. To me, this is a waste of time. If you are properly prepared for all of your sales prospecting engagements with a good elevator speech, product examples, carefully planned questions, value statements and objection handling skills, you are ready to close. If you are not ready with the above, you are wasting precious time.

4.   **Account ranking** - Over my sales career I have become a ranking enthusiast. Why? If we rank as much customer data as we can, decision making becomes quicker and clearer. And yes, I save precious time.

5.   **Account management** - There are so many great account management database tools available these days. If you can afford one, buy it. If you are really poorly organized why not try to work with a good database tool? If you do not work well in a database environment then make great notes and keep building on them. For important customers these electronic files can become quite large and valuable. Great account management allows you to look at your history with the account and your planning all at the same time. This allows you to make quicker decisions and save yourself money in the long run. Believe me, your customers are making physical or mental notes on you.

6.   **Goal setting** - Good goal setting in sales prospecting keeps you focused on your needs and wants. It keeps you in touch with the understanding that you need to make your prescribed number of calls each day. Goal setting also pushes you to make those critical extra calls that get you one sale closer to your quarterly and yearly goals and bonuses.

Time management is another form of big picture thinking. If you know you are not great at time management, build in the lessons recommended here and own them. Massage them. Make time saving traits part of your inner self. It will make you money and your customers will respect you for your punctuality, focus and tenacity. Best of all, you will make more sales.

31

COLD CALLING VIA MOBILE, SKYPE OR E-MAIL

Increasingly, the business community is trying to break away from face-to-face selling and moving these critical engagements to mobile, Skype or e-mail. When we strip away the ability to make direct eye contact with a potential buying partner, we lose one of most valuable EQ measurement tools. When we cannot see a person's body movements or cannot reach over and touch him/her, the conversation takes on many new dynamic tones. This opens up all kinds of mine fields regarding how our motives are being viewed and interpreted by our potential buyer partners. Many buying and procurement groups are using e-mail as a firewall or vendor fact checking tool. They send out RFP's (Request for Proposals), RFI (Request for Information) knowing this information will be used to keep their current preferred vendors in check or worse under cost pressure.

I could discuss this topic at length however here are my ten best tips when sales prospecting using either mobile, Skype or e-mail.

1.   **Be proactive** - I like to be the person initiating the call to a new customer. This is important, as it gives me greater time to get my ducks in order. There is nothing worse than being pulled out of an important business moment and then suddenly being plunged into a buyer call. Think of how many times a customer

calls up with a budget they want to spend. They pull us out of another deep engagement that is eating up all of our mental and emotion energy. It takes great agility and concentration to pull oneself into the present new opportunity.

2.   **Preparation** - It is also important to prepare for this call/e-mail in an extraordinary fashion knowing, if we get knocked off script or plan, we have as many tools around us as possible. Knowing our prospective customers are accessing databases and pulling range reports on pricing, it is vital that we keep up-to-date files on past discussions on pricing with all important prospective clients.

3.   **Ranked objectives** - There really is money in ranking our objectives before non-face-to-face sales prospecting calls. If we are not focused on the dollar value of each of our objectives in a ranked fashion, there is a chance we may overlook an important objective. Note to self, clarify exactly what the new customer needs and match that information to our needs. Look for opportunity gaps to fill with our products and services.

4.   **Monitor time compression** - Managing time is a beast in non-face-to-face sales prospecting. New customers can create an atmosphere of urgency by ratcheting up deadlines designed to force decisions quicker than normal. If we feel this type of gamesmanship taking place, slow the discussion down. Call for a break on the basis that we need time to review our best options on our potential buyer partner's best behalf. This pays dividends in the long run.

5.   **Cost modeling** - I am a huge fan of cost modeling, especially, for large or mercurial accounts. When customers are making large expenditures with our company, there is an expectation that we are always on top of their business. Secondly, if we know we are dealing with a detailed multi-level potential sale, it pays to be able to shift gears between cost models, on various products. We do this to come up with the best solution possible in a live setting. This is an advanced selling scenario. As more and more customers avoid face-to-face sales calls, we will be required to make tougher, quicker decisions to grow our share of a customer's budget.

6.   **Simple language** - My advice to Centroid Training clients who sales prospect using e-mail, mobile or Skype is to be very careful with the words they choose. As I mentioned earlier, we cannot see the other side moving their bodies or changing facial expressions as they react to our responses, to their queries. Avoid

any temptation to fit in a joke or a glib remark. These actions can just totally derail a constructive discussion. Stay with the facts and listen more than speak.

7. **Control your emotions** - Never let the customer see the whites of our eyes. Even if we are anxious, frustrated or angry, don't let the other side see this or hear this. It is a sign of weakness and the other side will feed off of this misplaced emotion.

8. **Note taker's role** - We cannot listen, think ahead and write with great accuracy in a fast moving big budget, sales conference call. This is where pulling in a note taker for the call pays off "big time". The detail which a note taker can pick up is so valuable. If the note taker is a colleague or superior...all the better because a person at this level can also slip us notes or prompt additional questions.

9. **Close positively with broad agreement** - Once we have closed out on all of the germane items on everyone's wish list, sign off the call positively and quit talking. One misplaced word at this point of the proceeding could re-open an objection discussion. Stop. Sign off and get working.

10. **We control the agreement language** - The last piece of any mobile, Skype or e-mail sale is the detail in the agreement. We always want to be the author of the contract if possible. It is almost impossible to get every detail in a sales agreement covered in one call. Be alert. Control this part of the discussion. There will always be finer details we would prefer to craft in the contract to benefit both sides, while limiting exposure to our side.

Limit the number of potential land mines and trap doors in mobile, Skype or e-mail sales engagements. This is what top tier professional sellers do naturally. See the sales engagement from end-to-end before getting on the call. Expect the unexpected. Be proactive and above all, manage risk in a constructive manner.

32

DINING ENTERTAINMENT TIPS

Entertaining important clients in a dinner or formal lunch setting is an art form. Food is so common, yet so complex. We all have to eat but, how each of us interprets food is totally different. When you add culture into the mix you have yet another notable dimension. On top of this, many people these days have more food allergies and sensitivities than they did in past decades.

Coming back to culture, you must take into account that there are just fewer than 200 countries in the world. The major culinary influences in the world come from China, France, Japan, Italy, Thailand, India, Spain, Mexico and American stylings.

When you entertain clients, you want them to enjoy and be comfortable in a dining environment, versus a trend point in culinary artistry. Understanding if your customer prefers a formal or informal dining setting is critical to a successful and memorable meal. None of us has the right to tell someone else what to enjoy. Therefore, if you feel you do not already have an idea of their preferences, make the effort and ask the right questions.

There is one more element to add to this mix and that is dining etiquette in the western world. Etiquette, some will agree has been lost, but should not be

Patrick Tinney

forgotten. It is not uncommon for business professionals who have accumulated great wealth to be unaware of how to correctly hold a knife and fork. Never mind, a flotilla of spoons, forks and knives associated with "fine dining, white linen service". Business dining should be taken seriously. Take the time to read up and practice appropriate table manners and social graces.

Here are several tips to consider when entertaining a new customer in a foody environment.

Clients' dietary needs/preferences - Increasingly, dietary needs and preferences are coming to the fore in client entertaining. For example, I have a friend who is deathly allergic to fish. Every time we dine, I go to great lengths to inform our server that fish must not touch the cooking surface on which my friend's food is being cooked. If so, he will become seriously ill and must be rushed to hospital immediately. None of these important details can be overlooked if you want to have a great dining experience with an important client. Do your homework.

The dining experience - Dining should be fun, relaxing, wonderfully paced, comforting and above all well beyond the prospective client's expectation. Make it so. Work with your restaurant team and plan where you will all sit to enjoy the visual experience of the restaurant, as well as its ambiance. Extra tip. If your client is a "Foody" see if the Chef will visit your table to check on your dining experience. Some Chefs are great with customers and this personal conversation lends itself to a great memory.

Reconnaissance - I like to scope out restaurants before inviting big prospective clients to dine. Go on-line and read restaurant reviews. Ask colleagues for referrals and recommendations. Find out what the restaurant specializes in. Visit the restaurant at peak period to make sure they are well staffed. Read their food and wine menu's. Visualize where you would like to sit with your client so, you can speak quietly and intently. Be smart and get in behind the restaurant battle lines. One more thing which may sound petty, but check out their rest rooms. If the bathrooms are grungy, you can only imagine what conditions are like in the kitchen. Note to self.

Business goals - There is a lot on the line in gaining a new client therefore, it is important to have business goals you look to achieve, during a dining event. In many cases, you can accomplish these goals without it even sounding like a business meeting. Make no mistake about achieving your ranked goals before you leave the restaurant. This will ensure you've covered all that you intended during

108

this meeting. This will also underscore the importance you place on your client's time and business objectives.

Plan questions - When I am in a dining setting as with all client meetings, I always pack questions that are ranked based on their financial importance. I call them money questions because if not answered, I may be leaving money on the table for a sales competitor.

Plan objection responses - Clients will not buy in a negative risk environment. Every business category has challenges it must face. All businesses have competitors. The market never rests. Make sure you are up to date on your new client's concerns in your business category. Be prepared to listen to them and supply them with information to address their concerns.

Plan trial closes - I love trial closes because as a sales professional. I can trial close all day long with prospective clients and not offend them. An example of a trial close is, *"What is holding you back from buying our products and services?"* If the answer is *"Nothing really."* then the client may actually ask you to deliver the first order just with an innocent query. The trick is to plan at least five or six carefully crafted trial closes. Rank them for efficacy and timing during and leading up to the end of your dining engagement.

Day/time/location - Ask for your client's input on where it is most convenient to meet you. They may even have a favorite restaurant where they get preferred seating and service. You must ask the questions or miss an opportunity to please your new prospective client.

Menu/beverages - My son cooks professionally for one of the world's largest hotel chains. I enjoy cooking and used to be a junior wine collector. SO WHAT. There are many executives in the business world who don't know or care about delicious food and great wine. If you are one of these food agnostics, approach the restaurant and ask the chef to help you plan the menu. The proprietor and chef will be more than pleased to offer advice on food, wine and other beverage pairings. When you take this extra step, you look professional. More importantly it will signal to your client that you care about their dining pleasure. This detail could be a signal to them that you will care equally about their business.

Conversely, if your client is well travelled and a wine connoisseur, solicit their input before making the restaurant selection. Once the location is selected, contact

Patrick Tinney

the owner or chef to discuss fine or rare wine pairings to match the acclaimed menu.

Transportation/safety - With drinking and driving laws in place, it is important to make sure your client has only consumed what the law allows. If this element of your dining entertaining is in doubt, prearrange a car service or taxi to ensure they arrive home safely.

33

HOW TO EFFECTIVELY PROSPECT AT INDUSTRY TRADE SHOWS

Sales prospecting at an industry trade show is a very different sales environment owing to a number of key factors. Trade shows are compressed into a very short period of time, usually one to five days. Second, business people who attend these shows have differing objectives and motives. Some show participants may only be there to see specific speakers, while others use the time to network and gather industry intelligence. There are a multitude of needs and wants to be addressed. Finally, there is the salesperson who attends a trade show to prospect new customers and even close deals on the spot.

Therefore, if you want to be successful in this action packed environment, how do you prepare to prospect successfully? It is no small task. Fortunately, I have some great routines and implementation ideas to prepare you to have the best trade show experience with the most profitable outcomes.

Elevator speech - If there was any time to have a refined elevator speech, it is definitely at a trade show. You want people to query your elevator speech to allow you to open a conversation with them, to reciprocate and ask questions about their world and business. A really good elevator speech has nothing to do the name of your business. A great elevator speech has everything to do with the value and promises you idealize on a daily basis. Do you remember Patrick Tinney's elevator speech? "*I help businesses make and save money.*" This elevator speech is begging the question…. "*How?*"

Name tag – Wear your name tag high up on your garment lapel or neckline in plain view. Make sure the writing on your name tag is very clear and easy to read. Everyone likes to refer to their colleagues by first name. Names are important.

Business cards - If you are attending a trade show with 800 participants, why would you not be carrying at least 500 business cards? The world's greatest salesman Joe Girard used to take boxes of business cards to professional football and baseball games. He would throw them in the air every time the crowd stood up and cheered an exciting play on the field. Joe believed that if anyone needed to buy a car finding his business card could trigger the sale. He had a whole stadium of potential customers right at his fingertips. Think about the costs in fees, hotels and food to attend a trade show. Now, think about the cost of a box of business cards. Think about what a lost sale means over a simple business card.

Presentation materials - Carry a condensed version of what your business does, who your major clients are and testimonials in your briefcase. Think about this promotional material as an elevator speech for your business. Save these promotional pieces for very important contacts you make. Make sure these materials point back to your company website, video and app. You won't regret it.

Rank speakers/panels - When attending a trade show, you want to squeeze all of the constructive learning you can get out of the time invested, especially, if this makes you smarter, faster and better. If this learning is cutting edge, you want to immediately apply this information to your business. Rank the speakers or panelists you want to hear and make sure you arrive early to the sessions to get the best seat in the house. Make sure you have a quick question for a speaker if they are not engaged. Strike up a conversation with people sitting around you. Take great notes in the session and make a point of passing business cards to everyone around you. No one will be offended and some may engage you with questions.

Rank key customer contacts - Many times, the marque sponsors of trade shows send their top executives to make small speeches before and after sessions. These V and C level executives may very well be potential customers. Make note of what sessions they are introducing. Make sure you engage these V and C level executives with a business card and ask for theirs. Everyone understands that trade shows are about learning, selling and networking.

Key customer questions - Meeting the President of a financial corporation, consumer brand company or media company at a trade show is a rarity. If you have this opportunity, will you be ready to ask a sterling question or engage in a great business conversation? Prepare yourself with the best ranked questions you can think of to link your two businesses. You have nothing to lose and everything to gain. Questions? What if you gain a great new customer because you were bright, bold and engaging? What if you smartly supplied this key prospective customer with a piece of intelligence of which they were not aware? These types of exchanges often lead to precious internal referrals.

Trade show networking navigator - When I attend industry trade shows, I am always on the lookout for a networking navigator. This is someone who has attended the same trade show for years. It could also be a sponsor and even the convener of the show. Keep your antenna up and find a person who can take you under his/her wing and personally introduce you to his/her inner show network.

Vendor trade show floor - As someone who is visiting a tradeshow, you cannot sell to businesses that have paid big booth fees to attend the show to promote their products and services. It is bad form to try and you may even get escorted off the show floor for this action. You can however place your business card in their draws and take their information and follow up with them after the show. The other approach is to say that you are seeking potential strategic partners in this environment, which, I believe is acceptable.

Work it - Trade shows are expensive to attend. If you are going to spend the money to attend a trade show, work it like this is your last chance to meet these new prospective customer contacts. Be brave, bold and inquisitive. Ask great high value questions but listen more than you speak. Have fun, but be gracious. Be proud to speak about your business but remain humble about your successes. You will be amazed how important business contacts will remember you and engage you well after the show has passed. If you want to be effective at an industry trade show, it is work. Nonetheless, I would say the work becomes more of a pleasure, if you prepare for the experience and the opportunities that will arise from it. Work it.

34

GOLF DAY ENTERTAINING TIPS

As a sales professional working on multi-million dollar accounts, I have planned and participated in a multitude of important client golf days with some very impressive senior executives. It can be nerve racking putting all of the pieces of the day together but, over the years, I developed a number of tried and true methods to reduce the stress so everyone just enjoys the day.

Remember, no matter what happens during the golf day, you want the client to have a great time. Let your prospective client cherish his/her memories of the day you took them out to play. This is what builds great relationships and keeps a sales professional top of mind with a new customer. This lesson is about entertaining with golf as an activity. A creative sales professional can take one or more of the following planning ideas and apply these tips to almost any customer activity.

Ten tips to consider when entertaining clients on a golf course.

Homework - Take the time to find out what level of golf your client plays. Ask if he/she has a golf handicap or best score while playing an 18 hole golf course. Also, ask how many holes of golf they generally play on a golf outing. Remember, some clients are pressed for time or only have enthusiasm for 9 holes of play.

The course - Ask your client about their favorite golf course or ask if there is a course in the area they have not played, but always dreamed of playing. Once a wish list of favorite golf courses has been established make sure you check out the golf course websites to make sure they are suitable. When in doubt jump in your car and visit the golf course and make sure it is player friendly. Be particularly sure the course is client player friendly. Some courses run on such tight schedules that they put every foursome on a clock for every hole. This can be troublesome if your client is a slow player.

The equipment - Some golf players play so infrequently, the technology in equipment gets ahead of them. Believe me, it has happened to me and I am an avid golfer. If your customer does not have the appropriate equipment, the Pro Shop at all golf courses will have the latest in rental golf equipment for both men and women. Good equipment makes the game more fun and just might improve your customer's game.

Golf attire - If there is any doubt in your mind, visit the golf course website you are about to play and pull down their golf attire requirements. I have personally seen this not addressed. It has resulted in a playing partner being singled out by course officials for not meeting regulation dress codes.

Locker rooms & course facilities - Take the extra step to make sure there are appropriately equipped change rooms. This gets you off on a good footing when your guest walks out and says, *"Wow what a welcoming atmosphere here at the course."* Also, make sure there are plenty of "nature break" facilities on the course just in case your customer needs to make a pit stop. Be prepared and be considerate.

Tee–time - Book a tee-time that fits comfortably into your customer's world. Make sure they are scheduled to arrive about 45 minutes early to get changed and warmed up to play. There is nothing worse than being rushed to hit off the first tee by a red-faced player's assistant with a parting remark to pick up your pace of play.

Golf cart - Unless your customer insists on walking make sure you book a golf cart. It will make the day much more enjoyable for everyone. Think about the setting. You are both in the same cart for at least four hours and able to talk about whatever interests your customer.

Food & beverages - Make sure your customers have food and beverages in the cart as you go out to play. If there is extra time, meet him or her early for breakfast or lunch. Remember, it is all about making them feel like they are having the best golf day ever.

Swag bag - It might sound insignificant, but I always had a customer gift or goody bag on hand. The bag contents can be as simple as your company branded golf balls, branded tees, extra blank golf cards and a golf towel from the golf course we were about to play. It's like a memory kit. Every time the customer sees or touches these items there is a good chance it will trigger positive thoughts of you and your company.

Customer tee preferences - I always made a point of letting the customer decide which tee boxes we will play on any given golf day. Sometimes they may feel full of beans and want to play from the back tees. Conversely, they could be tired from a tough week and just want to hit nice smooth shots with a chance to make a few pars on the round. Keep in mind, when you are playing with your customer, you are playing as a team. It is you and your customer against the golf course and the only thing that matters is that your customer imbeds great memories spending a day with you. A great day can go miles toward building wonderful relationships and profitable deals.

Implement these tips and you're off to a great start. Here's to the best golf days ever with your prospective clients followed by a few post play festivities. Your clients will love you for it!

PART 3
RELATIONSHIPS & TRUST

Patrick Tinney

35

E.Q. Versus I.Q.

How important are E.Q. skills (emotional, soft, intuitive, people skills) vs. I.Q. skills (intelligence, hard, process skills) in sales proposal presentations?

Edward de Bono gave us some clues with his creative thought mapping book, *Six Thinking Hats*. Edward argued successfully, I believe, that if we were able to categorize thought into White Hat (Straight Data) and Blue Hat (Straight Process), we could look at problems without emotion. He also argued that looking at problems or opportunities with Yellow Hat (Unbridled Enthusiasm) and Red Hat (Unfettered Emotion) we could bring our gut feel and wonderful sense of alacrity to almost any situation. Red Hat can also bring in a sense of uneasiness as well. It is a raw emotive state. Finally, Edward gave us Green Hat (Unbridled Creativity) and Black Hat (Devil's Advocate) to balance both E.Q. and I.Q. into a single thought process.

Soft, intuitive skills in sales pitches are largely overlooked or undervalued against the sexiness of cool terms such as, e-mail blasts and robo-phone messaging. Question? How did deals get started before Internet programmatic cold calling?

Patrick Tinney

Did soft, intuitive skills play a more significant role when we just knocked on a customer's door or phoned them in person? Have we supplanted soft, intuitive skills with stiff process that may be unbalancing our professional sales effectiveness? As a deal maker in multi-million dollar agreements, I recognized that I used my soft, intuitive skills to gain information and pull buyer partners closer to my objectives. I would do so by observing their voice tone, body language, energy levels, emotional swings, deferral tactics, and anxiety levels. I also prided myself on the types of questions I asked coupled with my listening skills. These are combined with a great sense of empathy and compassion in order to get deals done.

Back to Edward De Bono, we don't have to agree with the concept of *Six Thinking Hats*, but we have to admire him taking a stab at trying to create a new model from which to solve problems or capitalize on opportunities using E.Q and I.Q. transparently.

It's a little like training your mind to relax or ignore pain. It's just a style of thinking to lift us to a greater sense of awareness.

One of the undeniable elements of proposal presentations is momentum. Momentum leads toward tipping points. How do we gain momentum if the presentation pitch is just rigid process? We could argue that if our seller EQ is greater than our buyer's EQ, we have a distinct advantage in identifying momentum shifts.

Like watching great quarter-backs tell their football teammates, *"We are now into the two minute drill, and we are down by 10 points in the bottom of the 4th quarter. We have to raise our game."* It's so much driven by emotion as are great pitches that are tipped by momentum.

We need to incorporate softer, intuitive skills in sales pitches. If we sell something with passion, we cannot just turn off the emotional side of our persona when it comes to closing the deal. It just doesn't add up.

So the next time you are engaged in an important business pitch, take note of how the other side is reacting to your physical and emotional presence.

1. Are they quiet and just trying to make it through the process?
2. Are they anxious and overly talkative?
3. What kinds of questions are they asking?
4. How is their eye contact?

120

5. How is their body language? Arms folded? Stressed facial expressions?

What does your E.Q. tell you about your buyer partner? Is there an opportunity staring at us if we can just tap into their needs or help them through a tough deal making situation? Remember, not everyone hopes to make money on a deal. Some buyer partners are just as fulfilled by getting a deal over with so they can move on to the things that they do best.

Patrick Tinney

36

"You The Brand"

For years consumer goods companies and advertising agencies presented the term "Brand" in so many machinations it would make your head spin.

Brand at its root is an expression of a promise or set of promises delivered with great reliability and gravitas. Kings, Emperors and other Sovereigns would often seal their decrees and important political letters with wax bearing their Coat of Arms or other symbols of great importance. The overarching message was to treat this information with respect or suffer the consequences.

Fast forward to the settlement days of North America, ranchers used a hot branding iron to leave identifying symbols on their livestock. The unscrupulous, were deterred from acquiring this livestock without first paying. Big ranches had lots of help and lots of guns to back up their claims.

Today, brand has morphed into many different arteries of marketing but, at its root it is still just a promise. Salespeople are walking brands, and yes, we carry a bag of promises with us.

Before you place yourself in front of an important customer, have a look in the mirror and ask yourself the following question. "If I am a product will my

122

prospective customers buy me?" If you are true to yourself, then an examination of your make-up will provide important answers about your potential to sell yourself as a brand.

1.   **Our inner self** - The human condition is complex. We constantly process a lot of information about family, friends, net worth, health and well-being. If we consistently beat ourselves up, how do we expect to suddenly reverse this state of mind in front of a client? Conversely, if we work at living life in the present and are optimistic about the future, it will be hard to hide such vigor and vitality. Question? If you were a customer, who would you rather buy from?

2.   **Our expression of style** - How we groom, dress and accessorize is what makes us individuals. When we appear in front of a customer and ask him or her to spend money with us, do we inadvertently present risk or do we purposefully present the prospect of profit? Do we look like we just climbed out of bed after a bender or do we look like we took the time to make our outer self and our fashion sense shine like a rising star? I had a dear friend in business who was color-blind. He was a brilliant business person but could not tell what color he was wearing on any given day. Solution? He went to a men's clothing shop and asked them to put his shirts, ties and jackets together and number them discreetly. The outcome was my color-blind friend looked like a million dollars every day he showed up to work. Everyone complimented him on his personal style. What is your style and would you buy from someone who looked like you?

3.   **Our communication style** - I grew up in a blue collar city that embraced a lot of street slang. As a young salesperson, this worked for me for a while. Until, I joined a weekly newspaper in one of Canada's most affluent communities. I was hired for my alacrity and total hunger to produce. After a few weeks of my street slang around the office, I was gently pulled aside by my sales manager and was advised to shift to business speak with colleagues and customers. He was generous and was guiding me toward success. Guess what? I shifted gears, polished my communication style and increased my commission payouts. Question? Will your style of communication carry you to the winners circle? If not, address it. Remember, in our wired world of the Internet make sure your social media profile and the content you produce is constructive. Tough question? Would you hire you based on your social media profile?

4.   **Our confidence** - Demonstrating a winning pitch and tone in our presentation of a product or service is a combination of preparation and

perspiration. Great salespeople are always looking for an edge to make their product and presentation the best it can be. This constant tweaking makes future stars shine and industry leaders outshine the rest. No one can teach confidence. It comes from within. I would say however, if we have studied our products, our competition and marketplace with great intensity, we stand a better chance for a positive outcome with a prospective customer engagement. The old cliché applies. "Plan your work and work you plan".

5.   **Our consistency** - I have been blessed to have worked with some amazing clients over the years. We have collaborated on some wonderful business successes. Consistency and tenacity were my contribution. In my early newspaper days, I used to call on an affluent men's clothing store with ideas and queries about when and how we could do business together. Each week, I would prepare my questions and show up on the same day looking for an opening. Each week the customer would ask me how the weather looked for the weekend. Each time I replied that I thought the weather looked banner. He would reply, *"Sorry I have no need for advertising. Stop in again next week"*. After a few weeks of these exchanges with the customer, he asked how the weather looked for the weekend. I told him, *"It looks like it is going to rain like hell."* He bought an advertisement on the spot. We never had a sunny weather conversation after that and I grew a beautiful account with a great customer and friend. Note to self. My customer knew if it was raining, men would <u>not</u> be doing yard work. They would be shopping.

6.   **Our integrity** - Honesty is a nice word. Integrity is a more profound word. Integrity means, no matter how good or bad the situation gets with a customer, we will show up and make it right. This type of reputation in any industry will make us a winner. I have known a lot of really nice, honest people who were always in for a win or a tie. Truly successful people I knew, who stood for integrity in business became long-time friends and stalwart business partners.

Take note, my sales prospecting entrepreneurs, your personal brand promises matter. Your attitude about yourself matters. Your ability to speak to yourself as if you were your own best friend matters. How you present and communicate with your prospective customers matters. With this wider understanding of you, take your personal brand seriously. Seize the day. Go make money!

37

WORK YOUR NETWORKS

I'm a huge fan of working all networks in sales prospecting. It's much faster than pounding the pavement or combing through directories, lists and databases followed by endless hours on the telephone.

Joe Girard is a renowned American and known as the world's greatest salesman. He was widely acknowledged for his astounding annual sales delivery. Wikipedia reports that Joe Girard sold more cars in the USA than anyone else in his industry between 1963 and 1978. A whopping 13,001 cars sold at one Chevrolet dealership in Eastpointe, Michigan. Joe Girard has been recognized by the Guinness Book of World Records as the world's greatest salesman.

One of Joe's secret weapons was his belief in "the law of 200". The law of 200 simply means that nearly everyone knows at least 200 people through family, business and social life. Joe believed that if he could get someone to buy from him and they had a great network of contacts, this same customer just might be prepared to refer their network back to him. Joe actually paid people for these connections if the referral, was converted to a car sale.

Think about it. We all have networks. With social media networks such as LinkedIn, Facebook, Twitter et al, the possibilities can really become quite immense. Most people now have a combination of the following networks.

- -Family
- -Friends
- -Academic
- -Religious

- -Political
- -Sports
- -Kids
- -Associations

- -Business Colleagues
- -Clubs

The people in our own networks already know us and understand our approach to business, ethics and integrity which creates a huge advantage when we are navigated or referred to potential new customers.

My wife Connie worked in the corporate world in marketing and events for decades. This persuaded her to try her hand at running her own event company. Aptly named The Tinney Group, Connie set up shop in our home to keep overhead costs low. Then she set about building her portfolio of offerings based on her 25+ years of experience.

Rightfully proud of the great line-up of past corporate success stories, Connie prepared to sell her services. Obvious prospects included existing networks and industries most familiar to her. Unexpectedly, an opportunity surfaced one morning while I was dropping our son Sean off at primary school. As I pulled into the school parking lot, another father was also dropping off his son. We chatted about family for a bit and then I asked a frequent yet simple question. "How is your business going?" He worked for a large data storage company and he confirmed business was great. He also mentioned that his sales department was in the early stages of planning their annual sales kick-off. I casually asked if they had considered a theme for the sales program. Then, I proceeded to tell him about Connie's newly launched event planning business.

He was very interested in seeing Connie's work and creative ideas. His company didn't have a theme yet. The company was in the process of trying to come up with a real barn burner idea to really pump up the sales team. By the end of our school yard conversation it was agreed The Tinney Group would be navigated in to meet the President of the Canadian operation.

In their first meeting, the President of the data storage company and Connie hit it off and he wanted to get her working on their annual sales kick off right away. This was her first account for The Tinney Group and she was really pleased to be off to such a great start. Even more enthusiastic, when she discovered through her briefing with the President, there was a healthy six figure budget for creative, food, beverage and accommodations. Talk about blasting out of the gates with a brand new client. Unbelievably, all based on a Kid Network conversation between two dads and some very generous navigation.

Take note. If you look at all of the above network categories and then stack LinkedIn, Facebook and Twitter on top, what are your sales prospecting possibilities?

Remember Joe Girard. He is acknowledged as the world's greatest salesperson. And, Joe believed in "the law of 200". Joe believed in maximizing his network possibilities and you can too.

Patrick Tinney

EXERCISE 7 — WORK YOUR NETWORKS

Think about it. We all have networks. With social media networks such as LinkedIn, Facebook, Twitter et al, the possibilities can really become quite immense. Most people now have a combination of the following networks.

-Family   -Political   -Business Colleagues
-Friends   -Sports   -Clubs
-Academic   -Kids
-Religious   -Associations

The people in our own networks already know us and understand our approach to business, ethics and integrity which creates a huge advantage when we are navigated or referred to potential new customers.

Make two lists of 10 contacts. The first list of 10 is people we want to meet and/or be referred to via our networks. The second list of 10 is people we know that can connect us to the first list.   Once the two lists have been established, reach out and politely ask for introductions or referrals from these network friends.

Introductions I want   **Network Connectors**

1._____   1._____

2._____   2._____

3._____   3._____

4._____   4._____

5._____   5._____

6._____   6._____

7._____   7._____

8._____   8._____

9._____   9._____

10._____   10._____

38

BUILDING TRUST

Trust enters into so many facets of key account sales prospecting that, at times it can make your brain hurt. Trust is the heart of most business relationships. If you don't trust the parties you are dealing with, chances are, you will take extra steps to limit your risk exposure. These extra risk insurance steps can actually get in the way of exposing great mutual buyer and seller opportunities.

Conversely, if you are open to trusting the party you are dealing with, the possibility of collaboration gets brighter. Both parties may actually positively nudge each other to take greater positive risk in cementing new accretive agreements benefiting both parties.

While working for a National magazine, I found myself in the middle of an $800,000 sales proposal presentation where I asked my Sales Director, David Titcombe to trust me. In the same moment, I was asking an important customer to trust me. Talk about a pressure cooker.

I had just presented what I thought was a very strong proposal to secure the $800K. The proposal was packed with lots of value added and great guaranteed advertising positions in the magazine becoming of a top tier advertiser. Our customer carefully looked over our proposal. There was a thoughtful, short pause, and then the lead buyer for the customer team looked over at us and told us our offering was "just not good enough". I listened to the customer and reaffirmed her concern and then did something that gave my Sales Director "The Willies". I asked the buyers for a time out. I wanted to think about our proposal and discuss options privately with my boss. My gut told me we were close. I really wanted this deal.

The customer smiled and agreed to the short break. As we walked out of the room, David looked me in the eyes and said, "Tinney, I hope you know what you are doing." The funny part of this story is that I had called for a time out in the heat of the moment. Unfortunately, I had forgotten that we were in the customer's building and we had nowhere to go. We did find a quiet corner and discussed our options. There was a catch. When you are the one who calls for a break at an impasse in a deal, you must return to the table with a new and more valuable offer for the other side. Otherwise, you look arrogant and, in a word, dumb. This is a trust killer.

We returned to the boardroom table with a few new ideas to enhance our proposal. We got the deal done. We all got what we wanted. Everyone trusted, everyone won.

Below are five tips to build trust in buyer/seller relationships. Remember, trusted people get more deals done.

1.   **Listen to them** - If you want to build trust with a buyer partner, you have to treat them as a unique person. Everyone has objectives, goals, and aspirations. We all have angst. We all have a story. We have worries and bills to pay. Most importantly, we have loved ones to care for. If we thoughtfully listen to our buyer partner and ask the right questions, they will take notice. They will trust you more and more often.

2.   **Succeed with deeds** - Trust doesn't just happen in sales prospecting or selling in general. Someone has to start to build a foundation of trust. Someone has to take a positive risk and initiate the trust process. Take the leap of faith. Be the seller partner who says, "*Here is some information I know will enhance our future discussions.*"

3.   **Creative solutions** - Sharing creative ideas is definitely a way to build trust. Customers buy ideas, they only buy stuff when they have no other choice.

What new ideas are you bringing to your next sales prospecting client engagement?

4.   **Offer value** - In a sellers' market we used to say, *"Build it and they will come."* The problem with this thinking is we have been in a buyers' market for many years. Today, those who are buying want two dollars of value for every dollar they spend. This puts extra pressure on our point of difference and our value equation. If we offer true long-term value, they will trust us more.

5.   **Show up** - We trust personal brands not corporate brands as professional buyers. This means, we trust people, not company names and titles. It also means our personal brand as a seller is really a summation of our reliable, repeatable promises. When I engage business partners, I ask them one simple question, "Will you show up?" If there is the slightest bit of hesitation in my business partner's reply, I will ask for an explanation.

Trust is owed to no one. Trust is earned. Trust cannot be expected. Trust is given in good faith. How are you going to build trust with important prospective clients?

39

RELATIONSHIPS MATTER

A group of buyers I trained a while ago asked me the following questions:

Are relationships really needed? Should I be harsher in business deals? Am I exposed if I have a relationship with a seller partner?

These queries underline the pressure and tumult buyers face in the uncertainty of our current economic conditions. Buyers start to second guess their core business beliefs and values in an effort to excel at the bargaining table.

As long as buyers are respectful and have a degree of empathy for their seller partners, acting firmly or weak is just part of the dance. Compressing or decompressing time is just an everyday tactic used in a buyer setting.

There are dozens of tactics and strategies professional buyers use to unbalance the seller. The buyer's job is to move the seller off his/her script quickly. The buyer does this so she can start asking armor-piercing questions the seller may not have prepared for in depth. This helps pull the seller closer to the buyer's business objectives.

We must not however, leave our seller partners unfulfilled by a deal. Sellers that feel like they have been "taken to the cleaners" may start to resent a lopsided deal. Once resentment sets in, the deal will start leaking oil. Problems that inevitably pop up may not be handled well, placing the contract fulfillment at risk.

Solving problems is just part of business life. It's worth noting, solving a problem for someone with whom we have a positive, trusting relationship will get greater attention. It's more than just a problem. It is a creative process to try and help a friend in need.

At the end of a multi-million dollar contract signing with one of Canada's largest department stores, I made a mistake in a very quick verbal exchange with a buyer. It was an honest misunderstanding. It meant our side would end up banking $500K++ incentive dollars that my buyer would not know about until we were very deep into the contract.

I was really happy to have signed the contract ending a long multi-million dollar deal. Driving back to my office, I started to recount the mistaken exchange. I knew I had a huge problem. Approaching my sales manager at the time, I explained the situation. He told me not to worry and just wait for time to expose the problem and we'd deal with it then.

This didn't sit right with me. I knew this was a career-defining moment. With my sales manager's reluctant blessing, I set up another meeting with my buyer. I exposed the mistake and extended apologies. The buyer quietly mulled the situation over for a minute. He then asked me to correct the mistake in the contract so he could sign it. He also told me my quick action clearly saved him a lot of budgeting grief later in the contract. Problem solved. End of story. Well, not quite.

Years later, our company changed ownership and was embroiled in a painful restructuring. Many jobs at my firm were lost in restructuring and there were stories in the news about more to come. My phone rang at the office. It was the same department store buyer mentioned above. He asked me how I was doing and was there any uncertainty around my future. He told me not to worry. He explained that he had already started making calls on my behalf. Furthermore, he stated that if my job was lost, I would be working within days with his industry influence. Buyer/seller relationships matter.

Patrick Tinney

As a buyer, I would rather have a relationship with the seller than not. My reasoning is simple. I am responsible for how much the other side knows about the inner workings of my company. In this, my exposure is measured and calculated.

My goal is to reduce negative risk and raise positive risk with information sharing. As partners, we move toward positive two-way communication. I do this to pull them closer to my buyer objectives. Ultimately, this will strengthen the relationship and raise the spectrum of getting a long-lasting, smart deal done.

Finally, I recently polled some seller colleagues about being treated harshly or being commoditized at the customers' boardroom table. Almost all sellers had a similar response which was, "*Do I take my best creative ideas to a buyer with whom I have a good relationship? Or, do I turn to someone who thinks nothing of my company and has taken advantage of me?*"

The seller group was not filled with enthusiasm about the notion of sharing great ideas with buyer users and abusers. Buyer/seller relationships do indeed matter.

40

THE IMPORTANCE OF FRAMING SALES CALLS

When readying to engage in a large account sales presentation, it's a mistake to overlook framing the proceedings. Too often, I see neophyte, stressed or harried sellers rush to crack open proposals with new buyer partners without setting the stage for all at the table. It's truly a missed opportunity.

By framing the past, present and future dealings with a customer or a business category, we have a unique moment to contextualize our intentions and those of our company. In doing so, we also have an opportunity to check the temperature of the other side for their openness to cooperate and collaborate. If we don't experience cooperative feedback from our buying partners expect a longer, thornier proposal presentation engagement. This last touch with the customer allows us to shift strategic and tactical gears to fit the terrain.

There are a number of ways to frame proposals however, the subjects below are at the top of our list of must do's. This is our opportunity to be a spokesperson of all things good about getting smart deals done, that stand the test of time.

1.   **History** - If I have a client or buyer category history, I'll use it. Past engagement sessions with our buyer partners or business category can motivate the

future. By speaking to the history of our two companies and the successes we have enjoyed, we are able to shine a light on future opportunities. If this is our first business engagement, we can elect to profile how our business category regularly conducts and concludes successful, cooperative business agreements. The idea is to look for planks to build a solid bridge with our customer.

2. **Common interests** - By visiting common interests with our potential buyer partner, we are laying even more solid planks on our bridge to a successful deal. Common interests may have both monetary and non-monetary implications. Common interests may even include potential community building philanthropic opportunities. These community and B2C awareness programs create more mutual opportunities as an organic offshoot of a longer term relationship.

3. **Common objectives** - In citing common objectives with our buyer partner we are really asking a question. We are querying about closure of distance for the larger items in a potential sale such as price, quality and time ("The Big Three"). If when we speak to the other side about "The Big Three" we get positive feedback then, we know closing the deal will be easier. If however, we get silence or disagreement, rest assured there will be more heavy lifting to get closure of a smart deal.

4. **Spirit of agreement** - The spirit of agreement is really a nice way of saying "code of conduct" or "code of common courtesy". There will either be honor among men (meaning men and women) or there will be honor among thieves. Whether faced with cooperative business deals or game theory competition, it is always good to know there will be a framework for overcoming obstacles and blockages in a professional manner.

5. **Mutual opportunity** - During the framing process it is good to try to get a measurement for everyone to have a meaningful piece of opportunity. When framing this part of the engagement, if we get a sense from the other side that the deal will be lopsided in their favor, it is the time to suggest that we look at a bigger pie. By expanding the opportunity for both parties, the business relationship takes shape giving our side the incentive and fortitude to conclude a fulfilling and constructive deal.

6. **Determination** - There is a strong correlation between momentum and determination in successfully closing a large account sale. When framing a large business deal we really want to hear from the other side that they will see it through. We want to know we will both have "puts and calls" that will need to be

addressed and successfully navigated with everyone's interests taken into consideration. If at this point, if we get a limp response from the other side, we may be in trouble. If the other side is affirmative and enthusiastic, we are ready to go. We are well on the way to closing another smart, wise, accretive deal.

There may be some out there who think framing large account sales proposal presentations too theatrical or a waste of time. To those I say...a deal is not a deal until the goods have been delivered and we have been paid in full. I would also point out, that poorly crafted deals are bound to leak oil or may be unreliable in the delivery phase. So my friends, frame proposals smartly. Tell the other side they matter and that we care. Tell them, everyone deserves to make a profit.

41

THE VALUE OF STORYTELLING

An important phase after framing the architecture of a sales proposal with a new customer is storytelling. Participating in the media sales business for over 30 years, I observed some absolute masters of storytelling. Storytelling as a skill cannot be underestimated. Having the ability to bring history, creative ideas, risk assessment, cost modeling and logic under one common, sticky theme is wonderful theatre.

Storytelling is one of those topics eternally attached to business. I have great stories of wit, cunning, strategy and courage during the presentation of hefty proposals.

The question is, are there natural storytellers? The short answer is some people have natural command of combining soft skills. They think in these terms. They are curious. They naturally ask themselves and those around them many questions in rapid succession. They are also good at taking massive amounts of data and compressing it into a flowing stream of thought. This includes the anticipation of crafty sales objection busters.

Can storytelling be learned? The short answer is yes. Is there an identifiable structure to storytelling germane to presenting sales proposals? My answer is... storytelling is a personal style unique to us all. Notwithstanding, I will offer what I believe are nine essential parts of sales storytelling that we can start with and add to as we grow our storytelling skills. Storytelling is like building a pyramid. There is a base that builds on another base rising until we arrive at a perfect peak.

Here are nine levels of sales storytelling. Each builds on the next. They are dynamic so we can mix and match them to make them authentic to our unique, effective, storytelling style.

1.   **Our businesses** - The history of our businesses is a treasure trove of information to help build a bridge in a new business customer relationship. To point, a media company I worked for (The Southam Newspaper Group) was established in 1877 in Canada. One of my largest buying partners in media contracts was the Hudson's Bay Company (Department Stores) established in 1670 in Canada as a fur trading company. Can you imagine the amount of material I had to draw on for storytelling parallels between our two companies? Can you imagine how many bridges to success were built by these two businesses over a hundred plus years? Believe me it's a great story.

2.   **Our backgrounds** - Each buyer/seller seated at a boardroom table has a different background, heritage, lineage, education and set of life experiences. It's amazing to sit and listen to a buyer partner for the first time. It's like a door opens to a new world. A world filled with untold and yet to be heard stories that will bring two business participants closer together.

3.   **Our interests/objectives** - When new buyers and sellers arrive at a boardroom table, they each have a list of interests and objectives. These objectives and interests, no matter how close or how far apart, are the germ for a storyline in development. Furthermore, these stories are catalogued and remembered by the brightest minds in their respective industries, for future reference in buying and selling.

4.   **Our aspirations/goals** - Each buyer and seller has deeper aspirations and goals than are illustrated in a single buyer/seller engagement. It has to do with building a career and a body of work. Our work will be remembered and referenced by those that follow us. In building a career there is nothing more exciting than telling the story about how we landed the big deal. It could also be

how we shared our vision with our buyer partner for the future and how this positively shaped the spirit of business transactions that followed.

5.   **Our curiosity** - Our inquisitiveness about our buyer partner is the gateway to understanding what influences them in good times and under extreme pressure. Our questions directed to our buyer partner also give us the threads on which to build a lasting collaborative relationship. Buyers and sellers who feel a sense of ease and trust will do more deals together. The fun part is these partners will revel and tell the stories of how they managed those business dealings, for years to come.

6.   **Our inclusiveness/empathy** - Trust is one of the hardest things to build in a new sales proposal presentation engagement. Yet, it is one of the most important factors in how our buyer partners view us and our conviction to follow through with our end of a finely crafted deal. If we are not seriously listening to the other side's story, trying to feel their needs, aspirations and even pain, we are not showing empathy. Even worse, we are not really including them in our world beyond getting a signature on a contract. If we want trust in a business deal, we must listen to the storyline from the other side. Restate this story in our own words, so, our buyer partner is assured that they have been heard and that our words are trustworthy.

7.   **Our visualization/end game** - Our visualization for the complete end-to-end motion of a business deal is paramount to success. The trick is to build in storylines to enhance our ability to handle objections while gently massaging ranked back up proposals. Our ability to tell the story of how we creatively arrived at the incentive plan to close a smartly crafted deal based on our buyer partner's storyline is pure symmetry. It is art when wonderful deals close with broad smiles. That is the end game.

8.   **Our dedication** - When brilliant buyers and sellers conclude mind boggling deals, it does not happen without days/weeks of planning and rehearsal. When Sir Winston Churchill was getting ready to deliver one of his moving speeches to other world leaders to craft the best deals he could with limited leverage during World War II, he practiced feverishly on his family and colleagues. Most people think Winston was a natural when it came to storytelling. Winston certainly was a prolific writer, but more importantly, he was a great strategist who left no detail unturned. One of Winston's greatest strengths was his

ability to script and un-script with ease. He wove stories with conviction and great theatre. Winston remains one of the greatest orators in modern history.

9.   **Our masterful delivery** - How we deliver a storyline during a new sales presentation is the difference between being seen as weak or strong. It's the difference between being seen as trustworthy or questionable. When we are involved in large business presentations, think about how we want to close out on the deal. What phrases or value statements do we want to punctuate? What numbers do we want our buyer partner to react to positively? What will our final words be in what must be a truly compelling story for closing a smart deal that will last the test of time?

Question? Who is the greatest natural storyteller in modern history? My unwavering answer is Sir Winston Churchill. He was a storytelling genius. He helped save the world during World War II, one great spine tingling speech at a time. Winston accomplished this feat in an era where there was only radio to tell the unfolding story to the masses in real time. This illustrates the value and the power of storytelling.

42

CONTENT GENERATION & SHARING

Long before I ever dreamed about writing a book, I wrote articles about business negotiation as a way to give back to the sales industry.

I wrote short business columns on topics most writers in the business negotiation community had not covered. I packaged articles for release to the business editors of many business publications, newspapers and websites across Canada, United States and parts of Europe. Each release included the article, cover letter, my photo and short bio and of course a brief outline of my company, Centroid Training. These same articles were sent to sales leaders and colleagues listed in my database of contacts.

In the early days of building Centroid Training, writing business content started out to be a cost efficient communication tool. I was not only building my profile as a subject matter expert on business negotiation, I was also able to promote our training services. The articles focused on my professional business negotiation views and they helped to solidify a Centroid Training point of difference. This approach just seemed like a logical communication approach. I can honestly say that I had no illusions of anything other than helping individuals or teams become more successful with their business negotiation skill sets.

One day, I attended a luncheon with the partner of an advertising agency. We were chatting about how we might do business together. Then, all of a sudden he stops me in mid-sentence and said, *"You know I read everything you write."* I was a little taken back. I thanked him and tried to pick up our business conversation. He stopped me again mid-sentence and said, *"You don't understand what I am saying Pat. You are writing about business negotiation topics we in the business community should all be addressing but just do not have the intestinal fortitude to take on."* I was stunned.

Shortly after, I decided to Google my name only to find unbeknown to me, one of my articles had been published a year earlier. It was then I realized that content directed at my intended market, had the potential to increase my company profile.

I continued to write about business negotiation and send my content to publications. More doors started to open and suddenly I had been published over a dozen times.

I can remember sitting in my office, sending out my latest article on negotiation to my B2B e-mail list when an e-mail from a former media colleague popped into my inbox. He referred to the article I had just sent out and in his reply he asked a few questions about what topics I could offer to train his team. I noticed his contact information was attached so I made an immediate and timely sales prospecting call. It was 7:30 in the evening. The voice on the other end said, *"What the heck are you doing working so late?"* He was anxious to discuss an upcoming sales kick off meeting when he planned to train and motivate his team. My article piqued his interest and we agreed to meet in his office within a few days.

My new content based prospecting client and I collaborated on his sales learning needs. We shaped a program to fit his budget. In the end, I delivered a successful sales training program to a dozen senior sales representatives.

Now, what does this experience tell us? Having shared so much content with the market in a low self-interest manner, I had created a following and de-risked the idea of hiring Centroid Training. I had built trust, based on my business knowledge, career history and current views of what could only been seen as a challenging market for sellers. My content creation and free distribution had been prospecting and cold calling for me while I slept. I had been building a profile of my Centroid Training philosophy 24 hours a day.

Over the following years I was published over 50 times by a wide variety of websites, magazines and print publications. My next step was to take this content and display it on my LinkedIn Profile, Twitter feed and eventually on Facebook. This same content was posted on my website www.centroidmarketing.com at a cost per article accompanied by some free content. A significant amount of my content was picked up by websites offering free content over and over again.

I never planned to write a book. Nevertheless, I was being prodded by several senior sales executives to author a book on the topic of sales negotiation. Fast forward to 2014, my first book "Unlocking Yes: Sales Negotiation Lessons & Strategy" was released. Unlocking Yes continues to receive impressive, reviews from around the globe.

As a bonus, I had backed into a form of passive revenue through book sales that will follow me for decades.

My question to you is, "What ideas in your market vertical do you have resting in your mental rolodex that if published could work on your behalf?" Can you imagine if you had a machine that prospected for your company 24/7 around the world? This is what content creation and sharing does. This process of creating meaningful content and distributing it freely builds your brand and enhances your brand promises. It also has the potential to drive passive revenue on book publishing residuals for decades.

My greatest dream has always been that I would figure out a way to make money while I slept. Mission accomplished.

43

ADD MORE CHANNELS TO YOUR SALES HUNT!

As stated, I am a big fan of content creation and sharing as a way to add more girth to my personal brand and that of my company. Creating and sharing BLOGs, articles and columns is banner. There is however a level above this that adds so many more channels to your big game sales hunting. It has to do with webinar and video creation and sharing. We now live in a world whose openness for learning is panoramic. We also have a buyer and seller culture more open to sitting in front of a computer hoping to uncover great new futures via search on a variety of topics.

Here is my sales prospecting case for Webinars and Videos.

A.   **Webinars** - Webinars or seminar broadcasts in a live Internet setting are great sales prospecting tools. If you think carefully about your primary sales prospecting customer target, what solutions to problems are they seeking right now? What a simple query, yet it cuts right to the pith of why webinars are so successful. You establish a need in your market vertical and then build a presentation to share on this topic. You can send personal invitations to attend this webinar or you can simply extend a series of social media invitations via LinkedIn, Twitter and Facebook et al. I have been hired to deliver and have also used webinar settings as a great sales prospecting forum. If you are hired to do a webinar and

145

participants call you after seeking your advice or wanting your product and service there is very little downside. If you personally set out to use a webinar as a sales prospecting tool there is very little downside. Exchanging ideas and viewpoints through one-to-many conversations can be extremely powerful and cost efficient. You can track participants and call them later to carry on more personal and direct discussions. Lastly, webinars are commonly recorded for later use and/or for re-sale as valuable content. My only pieces of advice for you on webinars are:

1. Research your webinar topic thoroughly for originality and demand.

2. Practice your presentation over and over again until it is second nature.

3. Don't skimp. If your presentation has the potential to drive demand for your product or service hire a webinar management professional to coordinate and administer your webinar.

4. Follow up on your leads generated from the webinar. They are gold.

Quick story on why preparation and administration of a webinar is critical. A couple of years ago I was hired by a USA learning company to deliver a webinar on consultative selling. No problem. I built some great content for their market. The client wisely hired a webinar management company with whom I shared an advance copy of my power point presentation. The audience was invited and I moved to a hard wired land Internet line for safe delivery of my presentation. Brilliant. Unbelievably, just as I began to deliver my presentation the Internet went down. I was staring at a black screen on my laptop and a paper copy of my power point notes. Note to self. I was prepared with the printed deck of slides as a backup plan should any technical difficulties occur. I quietly asked the administrator in a live setting to progress the slide presentation on my mark. Since we were all connected via telephone and mobile I could still ask questions of the audience as I blindly asked the webinar administrator to advance the slides as I delivered my presentation. The webinar went extremely well. Everyone was delighted.

B.   **Videos** - We now live in a world that just inhales video. We love to be in videos. We relate to videos. We learn through videos. We demonstrate our product and service capabilities through videos.

I was doing my homework on a new customer recently. The prospective customer is forward thinking and has a great software product they are selling globally. To my astonishment this company had no video on its professionally crafted website. I was gob smacked. When I started my company about eight years ago one of the first things I was hoping to accomplish after I finished my website was to get a great video up there. A customer of mine, AV Canada, (www.avcanada.com) generously provided a video testimonial. They produced it through their sister company News Minute Network (NMN). I was indeed blessed and thankful for such a huge endorsement. I now have two videos on my website www.centroidmarketing.com. NMN is cutting edge green screen video production company. Check out their site at www.newsminutenetwork.com.

Advertising agency Greening Marketing produces a new video product called Brand Reporting (BR). BR is a combination, corporate video, public relations and news reporting all in one amazing format. Greening Marketing's BR is a highly successful video production company. Check them out at www.brandreporting.ca.

I cannot tell you how many views and compliments my videos have received. Videos do the heavy lifting of prospecting for your company globally 24/7. Videos can be posted on your website. Videos can be posted to YouTube. Videos can go viral on social media. If you don't have a compelling call to action video in production or up on your website, start working on it today. By not having video working for you, your company is choosing to leave sales prospecting money on the table.

Remember, we live in a global village running at warp speed 24/7. Sales prospect and make money while you sleep by taking advantage of webinars and advanced forms of video. Raise your sales prospecting game. Add more channels to your sales hunt.

44

SMARTLY NAVIGATE PRICE TRAPS

Recently, I read a column on client sales engagements suggesting one of the ways to navigate the buyer price tactic... "You are too expensive"... was to simply shrink the quantity of the seller's offering to fit the buyer's price. Is this a bad idea? Not really. The challenge is that price is so much more complicated than the option of a "scale to fit" equation.

Price is also about quality, time, brand, uniqueness, demand, supply, risk, innovation, competition and hidden value. If we are able to ask the right questions of potential buyers prior to and during sales calls using the above topics in the right combinations we will be much more successful at navigating price traps. We will also achieve greater clarity about the buyer's true objectives and intentions toward us and our company.

Let's explore tips and topics to navigate price traps in sales deals.

1.   **Quality** - The overall quality of our offering is key, relative to price. If quality can be adjusted then, price definitely has the potential to be adjusted up or down.

2.   **Time** - If we can alter the timelines to deliver our offering then, it is very likely that price can be altered. I once told a printer, his company could print our products on off-shifts to help him better manage his production time schedule. I just wanted good quality at a great price. We both got what we wanted.

3.   **Brand** - To some buyers brand means nothing. To others it is paramount. Understanding our brand and its positioning in the market has a huge bearing on price. Try not to get too caught up in all of the noisy definitions of brand. The clearest meaning of brand is.... "What are our consistent, repeatable, promises the market expects us to execute flawlessly?" When we can articulate our brand promises effortlessly, we will speak clearly to the market and avoid unnecessary price traps.

4.   **Uniqueness** - This is just a pretty way to describe our "Point of Difference". If we can confidently describe our point of difference, the negative price discussion stands a much greater chance of being neutralized.

5.   **Demand** - Markets of all types are driven by need and demand. If there is great demand in the market, expect prices to rise. In everyday life, think of the lack of fresh drinking water in many parts of Africa and the Middle East. At the opposite end of the spectrum, think of asbestos. Who uses asbestos products anymore?

6.   **Supply** - The overall availability of our product in the market has a great bearing on price. If our product is scarce but in demand, prices may go up. Think of Apple products. If however, there are too many sellers in the market of our product and not enough buyers, think commoditization and lower prices.

7.   **Risk** - Most businesses do their best to manage and control risk. High risk exposure usually demands insurance or higher prices. Conversely, low risk environments with little monetary exposure generally usher in lower prices. To illustrate, when in hurricane season in the USA there is always a chance that oil exploration rigs in the Gulf of Mexico could be damaged when these huge storms erupt. If storms are tracking toward oil exploration rigs at harrowing speeds, expect the market to price in risk and higher prices for oil.

8.   **Innovation** - Buyers love creative ideas. Businesses readily buy innovation which vaults them ahead of their competitors, even for a short period of time. If our company thinks innovation when it develops and markets its products, it can ask for higher prices in an otherwise stagnant market.

9.   **Competition** - The marketplace loves and depends on competition to keep prices in check. If however, we develop a product with unique expertise required to develop and service it, we can demand remarkably high prices. Not so long ago there was no such thing as a website. Most companies just used traditional media such as print and broadcast to speak to their customers. When the first websites were introduced to the market, financial institutions in the western world instantly realized e-commerce potential and spent enormous amounts of money getting their brands up on the Internet. In those days, there were very few technology companies who had the knowledge to write complicated code to power websites. A quorum of unique Internet development companies with great programming and database manipulation expertise created a sellers vertical market. These website wizards regularly tested just how much the market would bear for the build out of websites. It was a technology banquet where sellers ruled pricing.

10.   **Hidden value** - Many businesses have purchased equipment, buildings, licenses, technology and data, that are paid in full. In a sales proposal presentation where price is at the fore, many of the above items may be of great interest to our buyer partner and therefore neutralize the importance of price. Again, we have to ask the right questions to navigate price traps in sales proposal presentations.

45

SMARTLY WITHDRAWING FROM A CUSTOMER RELATIONSHIP

Entering into a new customer relationship typically means there is great potential for both parties involved. We savor the opportunity of gathering new wind in our business sails and pressing forward into new lucrative waters.

Unfortunately, for reasons generally not known, upfront requirements can stray into territory that at best feels uncomfortable and at worst makes us feel very exposed. The relationship horizon suddenly looks fraught with danger. So what circumstance would be so pernicious as to make us pull the plug on what we thought was a good opportunity? Below is a short list of seller/buyer scenarios of which to be wary. At this point we must count up our gains or losses and leave our buyer partner not to return.

1.   **Lose/Win** - I cannot tell you why, but some buyer professionals are so competitive they lose sight of the fact a business partnership is about making both parties feel like they are constructively engaged and not taken to the cleaners financially. The minute you feel that the other side is pressuring you into uncomfortable territory regarding pricing or future opportunities in a deal, stop and

Patrick Tinney

think about it. Think hard. Ask yourself if this feels like the bad side of a binary we lose, they win scenario? If so pause. Call for a timeout. Do not agree to a final deal until you have had time to review your cost modeling and your back up plans.

2.   **Lose/Lose** - You might think that "we both lose" scenarios are so rare that it could never happen to you. Wrong. Spoiler deals where everyone loses can happen. Think of it this way. What if the other side wants to do a deal with you so you cannot make progress? Your buyer partner may actually fear you knowing they cannot win with you in the long run. Knowing this, until they have a better plan they may actually elect to do a deal that does not make them money but actually slows you down. It's sometimes referred to as a strategic deal.

3.   **Profit** - If your buyer partner does not respect your need to make a profit, I see this as a big red flag. This is an indicator of "user mentality". On the rare occasion with a new business partner you may have to open with a test period of your products and services to prove their worth. Even in these circumstances operating without a profit is senseless and weak. Remember, after any test period you must return to normalized profit margins.

4.   **Cascade/contagion price erosion** - If normalized profit/price perimeters are not maintained, your company risks what I refer to as a cascade or contagion price erosion. Years ago, I was approached by a large client to lower our newspaper insert distribution rates in a specific region. I was advised if I did not comply, they would have to consider moving to our competitor. Against incredible pressure within my own company, I withdrew from that proposal for fear of price erosion on this account and others of its size. Years later, I was vindicated and actually congratulated for my courage in taking this unpopular price stance with one of the world's largest retailers.

5.   **Ethics/values** - If you feel like you want to take a shower after a sales meeting with a prospective customer, your stomach is talking to you. On the issue of ethics and values, always listen to your gut. At the very least, refer to your company's ethics and values policy. Once you have crossed the line on constructive bargaining or wade into the deep water of dubious ethics and values, it is very hard to swim to terra firma. It is hard to undo bad judgment.

6.   **Legalities** - I can tell you without question, the easiest deals to withdraw from are the ones that bring negative legal implications/exposure into play. Don't go there. A long business career is to be treasured not wasted on short term gain.

46

POWERFUL SCRIPTING AND UN-SCRIPTING

In a buyer's role, one of the first things I try to do is knock the seller off his/her presentation script in a purchase. This makes the seller vulnerable to questions they did not prepare for and opens up so many opportunities for the buyer to save lots of money.

When I was a seller, I can't tell you how many times a tricky or impatient buyer would leap ahead of my prepared remarks or during presentation of materials. The buyer would begin asking questions about my research or proposal figures completely out of the order or context that I had intended to present them.

Physically and mentally scripting yourself for a large or important sales presentation has a number of crucial functions and benefits.

1.   **Strategy and objectives** - Engaging in an important sales presentation without a solid game plan will weaken our ability to solidly deliver on our sales objectives. In large or important sales proposal presentations we must arrive at the boardroom table with confidence and the agility to counter unexpected moves from the other side.

Patrick Tinney

2.   **Creating order** - When participating in a sales proposal presentation with many moving parts and complex issues it's important to have a vision. How are we planning to bring this information into a flow best reflecting our goals and objectives?   Ranking and weighting key dollar value issues is important. Creating a flow for our presentation of the facts and arguments is the art in the deal. Flow urges us to present information in a manner that gets our points across without making the other side feel uncomfortable. Finally, this mental mapping of sales issues gives us a view of a finished picture or forward vision of a completed sale and/or contract.

3.   **Preparing for objections** - If we are able to articulate our objectives, there is an equal need to visualize the objectives from the other side. These two sets of objectives will reveal points of mutual interest and points where an expectation gap is evident. The expectation gap generates debate and sometimes objections. By preparing to listen to the other side and empathize with their objections, we create an environment where we can educate the other side on the value our proposal offerings. This helps define our unique point of difference in the market. If objections are handled professionally and with good closure it may actually offer an opportunity to ask for the deal.

4.   **Enthusiasm, conviction and momentum** - Enthusiasm and conviction are inner feelings. No one can teach us how to be enthusiastic. If we are well prepared and enthusiastic about our position in a sales proposal presentation, this builds momentum. In a big game sales presentation, if the other side senses we are legitimately confident, they will take notice. They give us credit for our preparation and will be comforted by our honest conviction. By lowering the anxiety of our buyer partner, we may actually draw him or her closer to our objectives and get a smart deal done.

5.   **Script to safely un-script** - Olympic and professional athletes prepare for weeks, months and sometimes years for a single competitive performance. This preparation strengthens their endurance and creates much needed muscle memory. It also frees them from having too many things to think about when they execute complex movements at high speed. Their goal is to visualize the routine and have a couple of key thoughts. They feel the routine without actually doing it. It's called "getting in the zone".

A version of the same thing happens with large or important sales proposal presentation. If we have examined all important research, objectives, goals,

154

arithmetic and foreseeable outcomes, it prepares us to let these factors rest in our mind as a few key thoughts. This deep scripting allows us to safely un-script and not worry about the unexpected. It allows us to totally focus on our buyer partner and the feel of the presentation venue. We zero in on the physical and emotion state of our buyer partner. We are so prepared, we are living in the present. We are "in the zone" to think and act creatively. This helps us recognize a buying signal and close out on a smart and fulfilling deal for both parties.

Remember, scripting and un-scripting in a sales presentation will help us make or save money. We just have to be prepared to recognize the opportunity.

Patrick Tinney

47

OPPORTUNITY SALES OBJECTIONS

Opportunity objections in a sales presentation are the gateway to truly understanding what a new customer really believes and wants. An opportunity sales objection is also what is standing between us and a great sale of a proposal. An opportunity objection is a blockage to a converted customer who is happy with a sales proposal and the purchase they are about to make.

If there are no objections in a sales presentation then, we as salespeople have become nothing more than clerks writing orders that have absolutely no stretch or positive risk associated with them. In other words, we are managing transactions of commoditized products.

Some sales professionals do not practice handling objections. Therefore, they try to manage this process by thinking on their feet. They are counter punching with customers, using phases such as *"we've already thought of that..."* This does not remove the customer's worries, but disrespectfully shelves them. To a degree, it makes the customer appear uneducated for asking a legitimate question with potential personal exposure. Making the customer feel dumb is not a great way to close a sale or build a much needed relationship.

Here is the way to succeed with opportunity objections.

1.   **Listen** - If a customer raises a concern or worry, they are doing so to mitigate risk. Listening intensely to our customers is critical. Don't interrupt. As a customer, if I get the sense my salesperson does not care about my risk, I will slow down the sales process until I feel the risk is in check. Or worse yet, I may just walk away.

2.   **Rephrase** - By rephrasing the customer's concern or worry, we as salespeople have acknowledged there is a potential blocker to a sale that must be addressed. It also means, we are getting a clearer sense of the customer's objectives.

3.   **Empathy** - Letting the customer know we empathize with their concerns brings us closer to them. It's a relationship builder. It's a trust builder. No amount of money in the world can buy trust. It must be earned and protected.

4.   **Query** - Asking well-crafted high value questions will get to the bottom of most concerns. The worry could be safety, financial or past bad experiences. We must uncover the nature of the concern to have any hope of neutralizing it. If this blockage is properly addressed the sales process can move forward.

5.   **Creative solutions** - Now that we have a better understanding of our customer's worry by asking great high value questions, we can set to work our ability to reshape the offer or proposal to fit the customer's eye. Think scale, innovation, service, quality, delivery timelines and payment plans. Leave price as a last resort and use it only if we remain profitable.

6.   **Collaboration** - Openly solving problems with a customer is the pinnacle of professional selling. It signals the customer and salesperson are opening their minds to arrive at a greater good and fulfillment for both. Collaboration is actually the "green shoot" of fruitful future and profitable transactions.

7.   **Our POD** - Our ability to truly express our "Point of Difference" at this stage of solving opportunity objections is what will separate us from our competitors. Our POD also has the ability to reduce commoditization.

8.   **Benefits** - When addressing an opportunity objection we are exploring the core of the customers concerns and needs with an array of solutions. Once we have satisfactorily addressed their worries, we are now able to talk about benefits. Not just any benefits. They must connect us emotionally to the customer. They must

make them feel safer, more creative, smarter, more efficient, relaxed and or less exposed. Think of these benefits as benefits on steroids.

9.   **Trial close** - If, as a top level sales professional we have guided our concerned customer through her/his opportunity objections using the above process we are ready and the customer is primed for a trial close. See if the sale can now be closed with a question such as "Valued customer…when and where would you like to begin to enjoy this great proposal?"

EXERCISE 8 — OPPORTUNITY SALES OBJECTIONS

Some salespeople do not practice handling objections. Therefore, they try to manage this process by thinking on their feet. They are counter punching with customers, using phases such as *"we've already thought of that..."* This does not remove the customers worries, but disrespectfully shelves them. To a degree, it makes the customer appear uneducated for asking a legitimate question with potential personal exposure.

Handling objections is about answering the customers need for clarity and/or more information. Keep this in mind as you write your top two objections and your opportunity responses.

1. Objection:_____

_____

_____

Response:_____

_____

_____

_____

_____

2. Objection:_____

_____

_____

Response:_____

_____

_____

_____

_____

48

PRICE, PROCUREMENT AND PROFITABILITY

If you are an entrepreneur or sales professional working in the corporate world and you are sales prospecting it really doesn't take long before you run in the three P's of Price, Procurement and Profitability.

The three P's come into play with different customers in different ways. In some cases procurement is not a practice you will encounter until you are prospecting in large budget accounts or contracts.

Notwithstanding, all business people who sell products have to be prepared to acknowledge or defend against procurement specialists whose primary interest is of the monetary value of a sales transaction. The opposite would equate to the value aspect of a relationship based collaborative sale with long-term business value.

As the three P's pertain to our aggressive buyers' market, here are some ideas to help you can navigate some of the choppy waters that accompany these topics.

1.   **Price** - In the simplest sense of the word price is an expression of value, supply and demand. The more your product is in demand the firmer you can stand on price and claim value. Conversely, if your product is in a highly competitive

business category, get used to the idea of intelligently speaking about price. Remember, price is part of an equilateral quality triangle comprised of price, time and quality. As each equal part of our product quality triangle gets pressured the other two sides will change in size and importance. For instance, if a prospective client calls you in a real panic, then asks for your product to be constructed in a special way and delivered in a hurry, you will be well justified in asking for a higher price. Why? The client has changed the base specifications of your standard product which could have customization costs attached to these specifications. Secondly, the client, by ordering your product to be delivered ASAP may force overtime or express delivery time. Both potentially incurring extra costs and ultimately higher pricing you'll be expected to absorb and need to pass along to the client.   Pricing is also an expression of our product's point of difference vis-à-vis our competition. Don't let anyone degrade your brand point of difference. Price can also be an expression of our category dominance and market share presence. If we have a huge market share advantage, there is ample reason to stand stronger on price. Finally, price is also an indicator of how your prospective customer's value your product, your relationship, and your ability to provide them with profit building ideas delivered with category leading quality.

2.   **Procurement** - Procurement processes established by larger corporations are installed so the buying community in these companies can act more carefully as they buy and negotiate for products and services. Often a buyer will predetermine the products and services required before passing the final negotiations and contracting to a procurement officer. A procurement officer may be the person who negotiates contracts rather than the buyer. Procurement is agnostic about relationships. Procurement always focuses on price and terms. Procurement will work hard to unbundle your pricing so it has a greater case to place pressure on pricing and debase your point of difference. The newest obtuse weapon procurement is using on sellers of all stripes is a negotiation strategy called a "reverse auction". This is a Draconian process where the salesperson who delivers the lowest price in a naked bidding war wins. If we are destined to enter into a reverse auction, our cost modeling and a profound understanding of the quality triangle encompassing our product must be crystal clear. We do not work for free. We must be profitable.

3.   **Profit** - It is hard to imagine a business operating without being profitable. Even charities must be profitable or profit neutral. If businesses spend more than they make, they will simply shrivel up and disappear under a mountain of debt. I

make it very clear with my Centroid Training customers that our company must be profitable. If the customer does not acknowledge my right to be profitable they are placing very low value on the point of difference I bring to the table. Furthermore, they are probably not interested in a longer term relationship. These customer indicators give us the ammunition to decide whether to do business with this client or respectfully decline. It gives us the strength to walk away from a sale having no substance or future opportunities. There is a great new book just launched into the marketplace titled "The Purpose Is Profit" written by Ed "Skip" McLaughlin, Wyn Lydecker and Paul McLaughlin. This book is expressly written for entrepreneurs, start-ups and small businesses. "The Purpose Is Profit" is a brilliant examination of why profit is critical to all businesses large and small.

49

TIPS FOR HANDLING AGGRESSIVE BUYERS

The majority of business buyers are generally collaborative, creative and sanguine. Therefore, if we have been invited to a buyer meeting we are there representing our company for good reason. We have resources to help create bridges for our buyer partner to reach his/her goals and objectives.

Pretty straight forward right? NOT SO FAST. WHAT IF YOUR BUYER PARTNER IS JUST ABOUT TO GO NUCLEAR?

I cannot tell you why, but there are some circumstances that just get the best of even the most seasoned buyer professionals. They can just flip out in what seem like normal buyer situations. The person who is typically the most logical person in the room suddenly becomes a 10,000 pound gorilla with an attitude. You could list a hundred reasons why buyer partners come off the rails and go ballistic. Here, I offer up my top four explanations:

1. Change
2. Exposure/negative risk
3. Big money
4. Budget pressures

Patrick Tinney

There are few of us who truly savor change or negative risk in the buying spectrum. So when new objectives and new plans creep into the picture the outcome can be quite mercurial.

When big money is involved, buyers realize one wrong move could result in jobs and careers being on the line. Big money makes everyone sweat and so it should. Budget pressures can make everyone ornery at the boardroom table.

Years ago, when working in the newspaper industry, I was approached by one of the largest department stores in Canada to lower our rates in a particular market whose rates seemed out of touch with the rest of the country.

In what was a constructive discussion with the newspaper in question, the newspaper advertising manager and I arrived at a rate slightly lower than their historical rate with this department store. It was however, not as deep as what the customer demanded. The risk was the customer could move their business and use this market as a leverage example to the rest of the industry.

Just moments before I was to meet with the customer, I received a call from the same newspaper manager, *".... Just want you to know your decision to lower these rates will be responsible for two job losses on this end."* Click. It was a short call. Talk about pressure I didn't need.

Still reeling from the angry call from the newspaper, I sat with the customer and presented our case for lowering rates as the client had requested. The rates were not what they had hoped would materialize. Not three minutes into this presentation, the customer stood up red faced and stomped around his desk. He threatened to bring in one of the very senior executives down the hall to really work me over.

My head was reeling. I was caught in the middle of what looked like two promising internal and external deals that were just melting down like a triple scoop ice cream in a heat wave.

In the end, cooler heads prevailed. I saved both deals and both relationships by getting everyone to agree that even though not everyone got what they wanted progress had indeed been made. These dealings were unnerving but served as great lessons for me in up-coming aggressive/confrontational buyer engagements.

Tips and Lessons Learned:

1.   **Don't over react** - If you notice your buyer partner is starting to lose it, do not over react. Let the verbal bluster and frustration blow past you. If you react, the situation could escalate. Don't let this happen.

2.   **Listen and acknowledge** - When our buyer partner is distressed and unloads on us it is best to listen and acknowledge his/her frustration. Everyone wants to know they have been heard. Once heard, the other side will be more open to hearing our back up plan to help them.

3.   **Separate people from issues** - Issues get solved at boardroom tables. Separate issues from personal perspectives. Sometimes people are under so much pressure, they become the opposite of their true selves. Always take this into account.

4.   **Like something about the aggressor** - When confronted by an ugly aggressor at the boardroom table, don't let your emotions take over. If they are using foul verbal or body language as a tool, stop. Look at your buyer partner and find something to like about him/her. You may even find something humorous about them. This inner focus on our side keeps us from sliding into the gutter with an aggressor. Again…stick to the proposal presentation issues. Be tight with your cost modeling and seek to close a smart deal.

5.   **Remain collaborative** - We just never know when a buyer partner is using guerrilla tactics to see how we operate under pressure. They do this to try to uncover any perceived weakness in us. If we remain collaborative without moving away from our objectives, we are showing enormous strength. This will gain us respect at the bargaining table.

6.   **Think futures** - While we live in the present and are mindful of the past, the future leads to great treasures. With the rapid turnover in staff these days, the person you are dealing with today could be gone tomorrow. If you showed great grace under fire, it will be generally known within the company with whom you are doing business. Remarkable calmness and stealth generally mess up an aggressor. These same qualities will be a strong sign to those who follow that we are sales professionals. We are not rookie "trunk slammers". It will be known we are not easily moved off of our longer view of smart deals that stand the test of time.

Patrick Tinney

50

REDUCE STRESS...SAVE ENERGY

Having participated in hundreds of large sales proposal presentations, I can confidently report no two pitches are ever completely the same. Businesses change ownership. Senior management teams come and go. Business cultures change trajectory. Category competition changes. Time compresses and decompresses. Budgets fluctuate. Mandates change. Civility changes. In short, trying to accurately predict how a sales proposal presentation is going to unfold with a new customer is a little like trying to catch a ball of rolling switchblades. One must prepare, calculate carefully, take precautions, and expect a little stress.

Below are several stress-reducing sales presentation tips that have worked for me over and over again. Hopefully, you will find one or two tips that will help you better manage stress during your next major sales pitch.

1.   **Prepare a proposal presentation planning summary** - In the last days leading up to your next major sales presentation, compress your planning notes into a summary of bullet thoughts. Get the summary down to a couple of pages. Rank the big money points. Frame your high value questions and trial closes. Highlight the pieces of the pitch that are critical. This last step of pitch preparation will give you a great sense of readiness and relief. It will take some of your stress

166

away, because, all you could know about the proposal in the time you had to prepare is now resting in your hands. This fine summary can be read and re-read in just minutes.

2.   **Stay in the present** - The precious present is where all the action is in a big money pitch. The challenge is not to miss it. We worry about the future and/or get stuck in the past. The present is where you see their body language. You see who defers to whom at the boardroom table. The present is when you catch that wonderful moment when it is time to "pull the pin" and say "yes" to a smartly constructed deal. You only get to say yes once, so don't miss it. Stay in the precious present.

3.   **Practice being underwhelmed** - It is so easy to get caught up in the lumpy noise of a sales pitch when the other side does not exactly get what they want and start to rear up. If this happens just relax and practice being underwhelmed. There are professional buyers who wait for imperfections in a proposal presentation to make unnecessary noise, just hoping to knock us off balance. It's a great tactic, but if you know it is coming, simply wait for the noisy tactician to make his/her point. Address the point, making sure he/she has been heard. Handle the objection and move forward. Don't let the customer know you even thought it was any more than an explanation of facts or collaborative motive.

4.   **Peddle backwards mentally** - I have found at times everyone seems to be moving too fast in proposal presentations and stress levels elevate unnecessarily. When this happens, I remind myself to visualize that I am riding a 10-speed bike and that I have a choice to peddle backwards. This lets the noisy traffic run past me. In other words – quiet yourself. Don't fill the silence. Let others do the heavy lifting for a while. Visualize you are peddling backwards while others are racing past you. The irony is that if you do this for a while, collecting your thoughts and analyzing the logic of the moment, you will be no further behind when you decide to engage those at the boardroom table again. The difference is you will be rested and ready to go again. Peddle backwards mentally to reduce stress in important proposal presentations.

5.   **Meditation & rest** - When you are in the most trying times of a large sales pitch don't forget to give your brain and body a little time out. Meditate if you can. You can do it anywhere. Rest. Close your eyes and try to think of nothing or think of a very quiet personal place. Or, think of your family at one of their happiest moments and how lovingly peaceful it was. Many top executives these days are taking mini rest breaks. Even a five minute mini break as described above will reduce stress and refresh you when you need it most.

Patrick Tinney

6.   **Laugh, forgive & forget** - A famous Hollywood actress was once asked, *"How do you remain so resilient and successful with all of the strains that go with being an actress?"* She paused and replied, *"I laugh as much as possible. I forgive everyone, and I can't remember a damned thing!"* If someone offends you in a small way in a proposal pitch just chalk it up to innocent error or crafty gamesmanship. Laugh it off. Forgive and forget. If on the other hand your buyer partner offends you in a serious way, forgive them, but take note. There is no need for a lack of civility at the boardroom table.

7.   **Dropping your jaw** - When you are feeling seriously stressed, try dropping your jaw one inch and hold it still for a minute. Dropping your jaw will drain all of the tension out of your face and will leave you with a great sense of peace. It works every time.

168

51

THE IMPORTANCE OF REFERRALS AND RECOMMENDATIONS

Referrals, recommendations, and endorsements are considered a gold mine. If you are a sales prospector, I encourage you to embrace these testimonials.

The question is, what do referrals, recommendations and testimonials really signify? Simply put it means one of our customer's has in a few sentences taken the time to put their thoughts down to express their approval of our brand, product and promises. From a philosophical perspective it is a bold act by our customers to overlay their brand on top of ours. In a sense, they are saying to all those who could potentially purchase our products and services that they had a great experience with delivery of our product, quality and value.

To future purchasers, meeting a sales prospector with a presentation, brochure, website, and binder full of referrals, recommendations and testimonials is a bit of a relief. It means the customers who bought the sales prospector's product had no buyer's remorse. It means these buyers were so satisfied with our product offerings that it actually takes pressure off of future buyers who aspire to do business with us. New buyers can move forward because the referrals and other forms of written satisfaction de-risk the prospective customers purchase.

Patrick Tinney

In some cases, prospective customers may actually want to speak to our satisfied customers. Satisfied customers can add in extra personal experiences and anecdotes too detailed to explain in a referral, recommendation or testimonial.

I can tell you with great confidence several of my Centroid Training customers openly encourage me to use them as go to referrals. These great relationships take a ton of stress off my potential sales training customers because they can call my constant referrals. They can ask them any questions they want in an open conversation well away from my operations. I have no control over the questions the prospective customer might ask. What I do have is a number of very satisfied Centroid Training customers that can tell their unique stories about how our training programs constructively impacted their sales professionals and ultimately their annual revenue budgets.

In a similar vein, I have written a book titled "Unlocking Yes: Sales Negotiation Lessons & Strategy". Unlocking Yes has been in the market available in Chapter's and Indigo bookstores in Canada and around the world on websites such as www.amazon.com. Readers of Unlocking Yes have been incredibly generous and to date have sent over 50 constructive reviews. This means 50 successful business people have placed their stamp of approval on my book. When I go to book signings or public events, I present all of these reviews in a handy binder for potential buyers to flip through. These reviews are precious to me as an author and a salesperson trying to shoot the lights out with book sales at every engagement. These constructive reviews and recommendations have sold more books for me than imaginable.

I want to wrap up this lesson by leaving you with a couple of thoughts.

Referrals - If you are pitching a major corporation or a large family run business and garner a meeting with the head of this business it is a smart move. Here's why. If you get an internal referral from a senior officer of a business to one of their department heads in charge of purchasing in your category you have struck gold. The person who receives this referral to meet with you has to look at your product closely and report back to the senior officer. Secondly, because you have an internal referral it is a signal to the buyer that the senior officer is potentially de-risking the buying decision. It is a Win/Win for both buyer and seller. It is perhaps your best chance to close a deal with a large company.

Recommendations & Testimonials - I want to leave you with one last thought. If you are in a position to ask for a referral, recommendation or testimonial, do it. Be brave. Be honest with your request. If you do not ask the question *"Will you recommend me or my work?"* chances are most business people will not think to offer. If you respectfully ask for recommendations, many in business will see you are a proactive sales professional and marketer. Most successful business people will smile either inwardly or outwardly because they all know how valuable these testimonials are to the recipient. Finally, chances are they have all asked for testimonials from all of their large clients over the years.

I love recommendations, referrals, testimonials and endorsements because they add another piece of important artillery to my sales tool chest. I am always proud to present these terrific reviews in person, on my website and social media platforms including LinkedIn, Twitter, Facebook, et al.

Patrick Tinney

PART 4
PREPARING TO CLOSE

Patrick Tinney

52

PIERCING QUALIFYING QUESTIONS ARE THE DIAMOND STANDARD

After World War II, business people went into over-drive inventing and building new products for a marketplace that had been decimated by the global effects of a massive conflict. There was such deep need that there was a gigantic build-out in infrastructure and consumer products. This type of colossal build-out creates a sellers' market. In a sellers' market, you have too many buyers and not enough sellers. In this environment, sellers have enormous power and leverage to ask piercing qualifying questions to gather all the data they can on prospective buyer's needs, motives, timing and budgets.

In my days in this sellers' market as a media salesperson, I considered it open season to ask any questions I wanted about customers' needs because, I had things they desperately needed. I would ask qualifying questions such as:

What is the size of your total budget and how much have you ear-marked for newspaper spend?

How are newspapers ranked against other media in your budgets?

Patrick Tinney

Who will be making the ultimate decision on what media buys get approved?

This sellers' market persisted for 50 years until about the year 2000 at which point there was a gradual shift toward a buyers' market. Buyers were taking greater steps and meaningful risks to secure greater discounts from sellers. One could argue that this shift toward a buyers' market showed itself much earlier, as buyers increasingly educated themselves on deal making strategy and tactics.

When the financial crash of 2008 happened, the whole global marketplace made a dramatic shift to a buyers' market as budgets from small to gigantic global corporations were slashed to preserve cash to prepare for 2008 after-shocks. This profound shift to a buyers' market meant there were now too many sellers chasing too few buyer dollars. This thinning of buyers produced chaos in many selling and pricing models. Generally, sellers are really not great at discounting while maintaining great profits.

Another equally important factor in this new buyers' market is that technology had and is having a huge effect on how buyers communicate with sellers. Increasingly, buyers are using Request-For-Proposal (RFP) filters to thin out weaker sellers. Buyers are also using databases and Internet search queries to gather succulent facts on products and services to make more informed and better buying decisions. The last and most devastating evolution of this buyers' market is buyers only want to see sellers on their terms and sometimes buyers want to conduct all transactions electronically. This is not good for sellers. All of this activity just eats up seller's time. It also reduces face-to-face relationship building time. It means we are further and further separated from our customers. Some buyers have gone so far as to use procurement specialists who take buyers needs specifications and then totally focus on price and only price. This hurts seller's ability to build strong business cases for their products and services. In this latter scenario a vicious form of commoditization of seller's offerings persists.

In some cases, this buyers' market is creating timid seller behaviors. In many cases, sellers are just too nervous to ask tough questions of buyers because they don't want to rock the boat in any manner that might get them excluded from a potential buy.

Instead of folding our tents on tough qualifying questions, I believe the opposite action is a must for sellers. Sellers must get to the core of buyers requirements before committing too much time and potentially offering the customer the wrong

176

solutions at the wrong price. Sellers have to become braver and tougher when faced with powerful, crusty buyers.

Buyers' market questions from sellers to buyers must be as bold as:

Who among my competition is in on this buy and what innovations have they made that I must match or surpass?

What important relationships in your company do my competitors have that I should be aware of and how long have these relationships existed?

If pricing is all that matters, how prepared are you for flexible quality, delivery and problem resolution from our side?

If this sales deal ends up in a reverse auction format, who in your company makes the final call on which bids are accepted and what recourse does our company have with your executive team?

All of the above questions are used to pierce new buyer opacity and neutralize unfair leverage from the buy side. As sellers, we have to use diamond drills to pierce buyers' motives, true needs and reliable budget expenditures that are bankable. Buckle up sellers!   Here's to closing wise and profitable deals!

Patrick Tinney

EXERCISE 9 — PIERCING QUALIFYING QUESTIONS

Piercing qualifying questions begin with the words, Why, What, How, When, Which and Where. These questions are designed to extract descriptive answers from prospective customers. These questions cannot be answered with a "yes" or "no". You can also create compound piercing qualifying questions as shown below.

Piercing buyers' market qualifying questions from sellers must be as bold as:

1. *Who among my competition is in on this buy and **what** innovations have they made that I must match or surpass?*
2. ***What** important relationships in your company do my competitors have that I should be aware of and **how** long have these relationships existed?*
3. *If pricing is all that matters, **how** prepared are you for flexible quality, delivery and problem resolution from our side?*

Keep in mind the above three piercing qualifying sales prospecting questions as you begin to write your own qualifying questions in this exercise. Design your piercing qualifying questions to fit into your sales prospecting world. Work and re-work your questions until you believe they will result in the greatest responses from your prospective customer.

1. _____

2. _____

3. _____

4. _____

5. _____

6. _____

7. _____

8. _____

53

BE CREATIVE WHEN WEAK

Selling from a position of weakness happens to many of us all on a daily, weekly or monthly basis. Selling from a weak stance happens for a variety of reasons:

- Scarcity
- Time compression or decompression
- Lack of knowledge
- Lack of technology
- Lack of funds
- Fear
- And others…

Sir Winston Churchill may have been the greatest seller of ideas from a position of weakness in modern history. He understood the above and he made the most of it.

Modern business learned a lot from Sir Winston and his battle against the Axis of Evil in World War II. Owing to Churchill's superb decision making process and brilliant tactics/strategy in constructively engaging the USA, USSR, France and his own countrymen what have we learned?

We can sell smarter from a position of weakness if we observe just a few of the following stratagems Churchill employed.

1.   **Appear strong** - This has to be the oldest stratagem ever, however, it makes the other side think twice. Remember the quote from Churchill's famous World War II speech, *"We shall defend our island, whatever the cost may be we shall fight on the beaches, we shall fight on the landing grounds, we shall fight in the fields and in the streets, we shall fight in the hills; we shall never surrender."* This speech put Britain's enemies on notice. We can do the same with our buyer partners but in less bellicose terms.

2.   **Show leadership. Propose solutions** - In his time of dire need Churchill ground out more international proposals requesting help for his British people than imaginable. At times, Winston had multiple secretaries working two shifts a day. By doing so, he was taking control of the narrative. He was opening discussions for deals on his terms and scope. When in a weak sales position we must ask ourselves…in spite of the tough spot we are in, is it not wiser to be leading the narrative driving toward the end game?

3.   **Build partnerships** - Strategic partnerships are critical for poorly positioned sellers. Britain was being smashed by the Nazi Air Force and its Naval Submarine Command. The United Kingdom's food sources were being sunk to the bottom of the Atlantic. The British faced the possibility of starvation. Churchill needed The USA to join The British in the War against Hitler. Churchill wrote, called out to and cajoled Franklin D. Roosevelt (FDR) then USA President to help save Britain and The World. Just prior to the bombing of Pearl Harbor, FDR moved toward Churchill in offering more than just materials and food. It was a long conversation, years in the making. So, remember Winston, when you are in a tough spot in a business engagement and need to develop a strategic partnership. Tip! Do not rule out your competitors as potential partners.

4.   **Sell futures** - With the British Empire breaking up and on the way to bankruptcy, Churchill sold key land rights for naval bases to President Roosevelt. Both leaders were cementing future opportunities. Churchill put in play one of his last bargaining chips to keep his country afloat. When businesses of all stripes face late payments or a financial squeeze, the first thing they do is sell futures. Think about how many companies Warren Buffett did deals within the 2008 financial crisis, on the basis of these companies selling futures. It was a Win/Win.

5.   **Admit strategic weakness** - Churchill secretly admitted Britain's military and economic weaknesses to FDR while boldly telling Hitler that if the Nazi's invaded Britain …the "Brits" would fight to the last person. This confession of weakness to a potential partner showcased Churchill as a savvy deal maker and a leader to be trusted. When selling from a position of weakness, imagine the courage it took for Churchill to pull the curtain back. Remember Winston. Be smart and sell wisely.

6.   **Get creative. Innovate.** – As World War II progressed Britain's factories, buildings and homes were being bombed to rubble. Materials and food continued to be sunk by Nazi submarines. Britain however, was innovating and looking for a new edge. The English were working on an infantile experiment with the idea of combining bomb technology, science and uranium. Part of Britain's creative pitch for more supplies was its Atomic Bomb Science, which it shared in full with The United States. Question? In a weak sales position, how will your company add hidden value with your creative innovations?

7.   **Sell fear/bullying** - Safe to say Churchill was brilliant in alarming the world that Hitler was unjustly invading his neighboring countries with a much wider and more malevolent plan in mind. I can tell you from personal experience if you want to mess up a large company you are selling to …just tell them you feel like you are being bullied with their tactics and that their course of business is preventing you from making money. This is especially so, if you can get to a VP/C Suite Officer of the company with whom you are dealing. These executives cringe at a bullying narrative because it casts a noisy light upon them. Remember, senior executives do not like noisy issues that are sticky. Many will fold like a tent and become very conciliatory, if you know how to gently push their hot buttons.

When selling from a weak position remember Sir Winston Churchill. Never give in.

Patrick Tinney

54

WHY LEADING QUESTIONS ARE IMPORTANT

A leading question is a question so worded as to trigger the proper or desired answer. If you've watched a crime or courtroom movie scene, you would have heard a million leading questions and some of these questions are so rhetorical that we almost groan when we hear them. A leading question example would be "Would you agree Mrs. Defendant that your nose has two nostrils?" or... "Would you say Mr. Witness that ears are generally used for listening?"   Brutal!

As a young sales professional growing up in the newspaper business I was surrounded and trained by some of the smartest salespeople in the business skilled at asking leading questions. Many of these leaders in sales innovation knew that if they didn't get the customer moving in the right direction in a proposal presentation, the whole discussion could derail.

Learning from these quizzical greats was infectious and fun. It was also deadly serious. We all knew that if we could not draw the customer into our bargaining continuum with great questions, our bonuses could be in question.

So, why are leading questions so important?   The answer is simple if you consider these question examples.

1. *Isn't it great that our two companies have such a long and constructive history?*
2. *Would you agree that our last meeting was right on point?*
3. *Do you believe that working collaboratively on this deal will bring us both to a Win/Win agreement?*
4. *Could we say that our relationship has always been the basis for our on-going ability to close solid deals?*

The neat thing about all of the above questions is that on the surface they are innocuous. The questions are meant to put the customer at ease, while paving the way to meatier questions further down steam in the deal. These non-threatening questions while leading to effortless "yes's" on the customer's part also confirm there are no underlying problems with the customer's perception of our ongoing relationship and performance.

If for any reason the customer says "no" to any of the above questions it is time to slow the discussion down. Ask deeper high value questions to address any concerns the customer has about our collaborative future. This is a critical point because if the customer wants to air some objections or complaints, this is the time to catch them and listen to them closely. Remember, no matter how small the issue or objection the customer has, we must take the time to hear them out. We must do this because as intelligent business people, we all want to be heard. We want to be reassured that the decisions we are about to make are the smartest and best available.

Now, get working on your leading questions! And, here's to guiding your sales proposal presentations to wise and profitable closure! "It's fun to sign large deals....wouldn't you say?"

EXERCISE 10 — PROPOSAL PRESENTATIONS LEADING QUESTIONS

We use leading questions in sales proposal presentations to create much needed positive momentum.

One of the best ways to start leading questions in a sales proposal presentation is to talk about the relationship, history, past success or common objectives that a customer and salesperson have or will benefit both partners. Here is a solid list of proposal presentations leading questions:

1. *Isn't it great that our two companies have such a long and constructive history?*

2. *Would you agree that our last meeting was right on point?*

3. *Do you believe that working collaboratively on this deal will bring us both to a Win/Win agreement?*

4. *Could we say that our relationship has always been the basis for our on-going ability to close solid deals?*

Keep in mind the above four leading sales prospecting questions as you begin to write your own leading questions. Design your leading questions to fit into your sales prospecting world. Work and re-work your questions until you believe they will result in the greatest momentum moving your customer to confident "yes's".

1. _____

2. _____

3. _____

4. _____

5. _____

6. _____

55

IDENTIFYING AND NAVIGATING AN IMPASSE

An impasse tells us the structural nature of a proposal is perceived as being flawed, lopsided or undoable by one or both parties in a sales presentation. It could be a deadlock on price, time, quality, service or other factors. If we dig past the intellectual side of the discussion, the impasse has strong emotional underpinnings.

When we reach an impasse in a sales proposal presentation with a customer we could be thinking any of the following:

1. Why can't you see my side?
2. You just don't get it.
3. You are taking advantage of our relationship.
4. You are hiding something.
5. I no longer trust you and I am fearful of your intentions.
6. Can we find someone else to replace this business partner?
7. Can we just walk away from this business partner?

Pretty ugly. This is more common than you think especially in a stagnant or deflationary economy. Not only do we have the above emotional side of the

Patrick Tinney

discussion but, we also have the tactical side of how it all happened. Don't rule out buyer egos running amuck.

In its most rudimentary form, a sales proposal impasse is telling the buyer participants that they are no longer in their "comfort zone" to get a deal done. At Centroid Training we call the comfort zone "The Bargaining Continuum".

When we are in the bargaining continuum there is hope an opportunity will arise to engage in bargaining reciprocity to close a smart and fulfilling deal for both parties.

It's impractical to think your company will be able to avoid proposal impasses with business partners. Here are some tips that will help your company better navigate an impasse in sales proposal presentations.

1. Conduct reconnaissance on your buyer partner's world. Gain as much intelligence on them as possible. By understanding more about their business, and their future, your company stands a much better chance of signing smart, sustainable deals.
2. Rank and weigh objectives for your company and theirs. Next, understand their objectives and know what they really need combined with the clarity of what you really need. This knowledge will have greater opportunity to pull the other side closer to you. This action will help close the expectation gap that comes with all sales proposals. This process lowers negative risk.
3. Next, there is the spirit of the deal. We must learn to listen and have appreciation for the other side, even when we'd rather not. No empathy?? Sorry, not likely to get a sustainable deal done.
4. Be realistic with cost demands. If you are low balling or hard balling, what do you expect the other side to do? How can we honestly expect to lower our costs by raising our buyer partner's costs? Creative soft cost proposals from our side will add value for them. This may help offset some costs for the other side.
5. Make your proposals simple, understandable and accessible. If your buyer partner cannot clearly understand the details and benefits of your proposal, it will only slow the sales process down. Yep, you guessed it; this will start the ball rolling toward an impasse.
6. Have a backup plan. Have several back up plans if you like. You can say "no" politely as often as you like in discussing a business deal and

generally not offend the other side. Just be careful not to say "no never". Remember, never is a long, long time and leaves you no outs.

7. Most sales proposal impasses are avoidable. The key is having a sales proposal thought process that works to lower relationship risk while still trying to get smart deals done.

56

WIN MORE SALES WITH VALUE STATEMENTS

Most proposal presentations progress smoothly, largely because two parties have found enough common ground to take time to listen to each other's needs and aspirations. Most customers do extensive homework on their suppliers to mitigate risk and to understand the suppliers' point of difference or unique vertical within their business category.

If all goes well, both parties carefully explain the objectives within their needs. Generally, an expectation gap is identified by both buyers and sellers. Some kind of give and take commences to bring about amicable closure of a deal.

In tougher buyer discussions, savvy customers will do their best to knock sellers off their script and throw out creative objections. Sharp queries appear to double check their known facts and back check our claims. Seasoned sales proposal prospectors expect to be put to the test and are prepared to answer "burden of proof questions". It's just part of the process.

Sellers have been trained to handle a wide variety of objections from customers. If they handle these objections constructively, the sales presentation just gets back on course and the deal closes out with a solid Win/Win agreement.

In spite of all of the above, some sales presentations just get bogged down in objections that are not fully satisfied with convincing answers to them. Somehow elements of doubt enter the discussion and the sale stalls. So, how does this happen? Typically, there is a missing step – the value statement.

Value statements are a bridge between the skillful handling of a customer objection and a trial close. Value statements are an overarching truth about a seller's brand prominence in their business category that helps solidify their position for longer term relationships with larger customers.

Value statements are designed to help reassure a customer the experience they will have with our product or service has been enjoyed by many of the prospective customer's contemporaries. These experiences are constructive and accretive.

Value statements acknowledging a customer concern/objection sound like this:

1. *"The reason our large customers purchase our products year after year is because our delivery and post-delivery follow-up is second to none."*

2. *"The reason we get so many product trials with our large customers is because we vigorously back test the products to mitigate negative risk."*

3. *"The reason our large customers come to us first with problems or opportunities is because they know we have a great creative team working tirelessly to create unique solutions for unique customers."*

As we see from the above examples, value statements are "truth and positive affirmation *because* statements". Value statements are the bridge between skillfully handled customers objections and masterful trial close questions. Value statements put the customer at ease knowing that the seller and their company stand behind their promises and that they have lived their brand. Value statements are an affirmation of the reliable repeatable promises for which your company is proudly recognized.

So be smart. Incorporate value statements into your next sales proposal presentation when the going gets tough. Your customers will appreciate that you are listening to them. And, that you and your company care.

Remember, large customers not only want great long-term relationships, they want to know that your company will show up and live up to its promises rain or shine.

Patrick Tinney

EXERCISE 11 — VALUE STATEMENTS

Value statements are "truth and positive affirmation <u>because</u> statements". Value statements are the bridge between skillfully handled customers objections and masterful trial close questions. Value statements put the customer at ease, knowing the seller and her company stand behind their promises and have lived their brand. Value statements are an affirmation of the reliable repeatable promises your company stands behind.

1. *"The reason our large customers purchase our products year after year is <u>because</u> our delivery and post-delivery follow-up is second to none."*
2. *"The reason we get so many product trials with our large customers is <u>because</u> we vigorously back test the products to mitigate negative risk."*
3. *"The reason our large customers come to us first with problems or opportunities is <u>because</u> they know we have a great creative team working tirelessly to create unique solutions for unique customers."*

Review the above three value statements as you begin to write your own value statements. Design your *because* statements to fit into your sales prospecting world. Work and re-work your statements until you believe they will result in the greatest insight and response from your prospective customer.

1. _____

2. _____

3. _____

4. _____

5. _____

6. _____

57

EFFECTIVE TRIAL CLOSES

At a gathering, I asked a relative in my wife's family who once owned a large car dealership what the best piece of deal closing advice he had received over his storied career. He took his time to respond and said, *"Yes I remember it well. A giant in the auto industry once told me that to be successful in car sales, I had to visualize that I was always standing in a round room."* He had passed along a gem that remains with me today and a quote that I often use in our Centroid Training sessions. Metaphorically, he was saying, take the corners out of the room so you have room to back up and regroup.

One of the themes I like to leave with our Centroid Training graduates is that nicely crafted questions delivered politely are innocuous. We can ask tons of carefully crafted questions in our pursuit of a "yes". An example of a trial close question is "What would it take to get this deal done?"

The alternative is to ask a question in a hard, closed ended fashion. An example of a closed question is…. "Do we have a deal?" This small question might seem like a risk free question in the closing stages of a business deal but, it isn't. By asking this direct question we have initiated a "coin toss" result. The answer will ultimately lead to a "yes or no". This means, by questioning in this direct manner

I've opened up a 50% chance of a "no" in the overarching sales deal. I have inadvertently backed myself into a corner, by asking this question so directly.

Let's get back to visualizing we are operating in a round room in the closing phases of a sales deal. By asking a direct question, I have senselessly built a corner where there was none. I am boxing myself in. Question? Is there an appropriate time to directly ask for the deal? Yes there is. The time to directly ask for the deal is when you have exhausted all lower risk trial close questions including our examples below and or when you are running out of time.

Ask trial close questions similar to these examples:

1. ***Where*** *would you like to begin our proposal?*

2. ***When*** *is the best time to initiate this proposal?*

3. ***What*** *about this proposal do you like and* ***which*** *of your stakeholders would like it too?*

4. ***Which*** *group in your organization would benefit most from our proposal?*

5. ***How*** *do you visualize closing out this deal?*

Trial closes are a thing of beauty because they do all of the heavy lifting a direct close does without boxing us in. Additionally, if we are in collaboration mode with your new customer, the customer may actually offer up valuable information. In a better case scenario, they actually share creative approaches they visualize on the potential deal. The customer may even start to sell us on his/her ideas to get final closure of the deal. In the best case scenario, they say, *"You know we've really discussed the opportunities and exposed the risk in this proposal. I think there are more positives than negatives. Let's sign this deal and get going."*

Centroid Training participants learn that trial close questions are money questions and I sincerely believe this. When heading into an important sales presentation rank your trial close questions for dollar value and effect. Think about how much time you have in an important sales proposal presentation with senior executive buyer? The answer is, not much. Craft your trial close questions carefully. Rank them. Practice them. Role play with them. The better you get at delivering trial close questions in pressure cooker sales presentation situations, the more deals you will close with the lowest amount of risk.

EXERCISE 12 — EFFECTIVE TRIAL CLOSE QUESTIONS

The trial close examples noted here are very similar to a "high value" questions. High value questions are questions beginning with specific words such as; "Who, Why, Where, When, Which, Where and How". So what is the difference between a high value question and a trial close? The answer is it has to do with tightening the scope of our query toward the end of a deal making session. Trial close questions are used to surgically expose blockages or impediments to the deal closing. Trial closes are also used to trigger spontaneous closure by the customer. Trial close questions also tend to steer toward opportunities in Timing, Place, Utility, Profitability, Success, Approval and Authority.

1. *Where would you like to begin our proposal?*

2. *When is the best time to initiate this proposal?*

3. *What about this proposal do you like and which of your stakeholders would like it too?*

4. *Which group in your organization would benefit most from our proposal?*

5. *How do you visualize closing out this deal?*

Keep in mind the above five trial close sales prospecting questions as you begin to write your own trial close questions. Design your trial close questions to fit into your sales prospecting world. Work and re-work your questions until you believe they will result in the greatest response from your prospective customer to close wise and profitable deals.

1. _____

2. _____

3. _____

4. _____

5. _____

58

How Sales Professionals "Close New Deals"

I get totally focused once the proceedings of a proposal have been properly framed. Once we have general agreement, buyer and seller start moving more confidently toward closure of a mutually beneficial deal.

The closure of a new sales deal can happen in dozens of different ways depending on how much budget is involved and how complicated the components of a deal reveal. Generally, in larger deals there is almost a cadence or process many in business will expect and recognize. It is generally not a rushed affair unless the customer makes it so. It almost has the feeling of a train starting up its engines.

When I am closing out a deal, I want to pass a series of check points and bolt down all of the pieces of the deal before the train leaves the station. Whenever possible, I want to be the engineer of the train as it picks up speed on route to its closure and profitable destination. Here are the check points in a profitable deal closure I want you as a sales professional or entrepreneur to pay extra close attention to.

Positions tabled - We always start the close of a deal with all positions that have been tabled in the deal. We do this to be sure there have been no changes in the hours or days leading up to this last meeting.

Build a bridge - We lay the planks of a bridge in a deal by starting with the elements of the deal that everyone one agrees on. We may even use a leading question to prompt the proceedings such as, *"I think (buyer partner) that you'd agree we are simpatico on the following list of items."* We do this for two reasons. First, we get the new customer to say "yes". We want the customer to get used to saying yes because this builds much needed momentum to get the deal done. Second, if there is any hesitation, this is the moment to address it and move on with greater confidence.

Lower cost items - Next by addressing lower cost items in the sale, we are building even more momentum and laying more planks in our bridge. Broad agreement as this point means we just have one big hurdle left.

Tough stuff - The last elements of a deal almost always have to do with price, quality and time. If we have listened clearly to our customer's needs and motives, our cost modeling and the incentive elements of our proposal do the heavy lifting here. If you get bogged down a bit with the customer over sticking points just remain calm. Act underwhelmed as if you expected this last tactical move from the customer. Once this bump has been cleared and we have broad smiles again, we start to really zero in on the close

Re-cap - It is always wise to do a short re-cap of the deal just as a final touch point to make sure all major points in our proposal have been accepted in their various forms.

Ask for deal - We close by stating, *"If there are no outstanding items I believe we have a deal!"*

Finish deal upbeat - Always finish positively even if the last part of the deal was a bit of a hand wringer. Stay calm. Shake hands with your new customer. Smile and leave the building.

Stop selling - Why leave the building if you have a deal? Why? Simply because every extra word we speak as sellers after a deal has been closed increases the risk of unnecessarily re-opening the deal or even worse, losing the deal. I have seen deals actually close and the seller could not stop talking and continued to give more profit away unnecessarily and even recklessly. Note to self. Stop selling. Leave the building.

We draft contract - Once a deal has been struck, stop and capture the last details of your final meeting. If it is a very important deal, this is where having a note

Patrick Tinney

taker with you pays big time. The seller always wants to be the one who drafts the contract to be signed. There is a simple reason for this. Small details that did not get covered in the deal then become your responsibility. Interpret them as you remembered them and write the details in the written contract. This is where smart sellers reduce their exposure to buyers who might want to ask for add-ons not documented in the contract. This is also the part where you may want to control terms of payment. Everyone has their own view on what is important in these small details.

Parties sign-off - Once the contract has been drafted it is simply a formality of getting the agreement signed and dated by both parties. Is this important? In a word "yes". What if the person you just shook hands with on a deal gets sick or leaves the company? The contract speaks for that person in their absence and stands as a living document.

Last thoughts – If the products and services you sell are straight forward, use the pieces of the close-out process described above to best fit your business model. If your contracts are iron clad and clearly spelled out, you are in a position to ask for the sale and just close-out.

Closing-out a deal is perhaps the most exciting part of sale. It promises great beginnings and profitable futures for both buyer and seller. Pay close attention to the tips I have offered you here. Signing important contacts is like winning a game of chess. If you can do it once successfully, you can do it over and over growing your sales confidence and business profitably for many years to come.

PART 5
THE AFTERMATH

Patrick Tinney

59

THE VALUE OF POST MORTEM IN SALES PROPOSAL PRESENTATIONS

All great sales professionals look to their victories and stinging loses for inspiration in future sales engagements. A post mortem of any sales proposal presentation will always reveal a treasure trove of new and valuable information.

Sales professionals immediately prepare for the next presentation by capturing every detail of the sales proposal presentation they have just delivered. They make copious notes on all topics from the sales pitch. Seasoned sales professionals may take weeks to discreetly probe their buyer partners to garner even more information and to draw final conclusions on how they will prepare for and execute their next engagement. The short line is "learn from your experiences".

Sales professionals go to these great lengths because, like great chess masters each opponent they engage has a specific line of thought as they lay out their buyer plans. Our buyer partner's logic base may repeat itself. For example, they may choose a specific time of day to meet, to enhance their access to information. They may like to meet in the morning when they are most uncluttered mentally and most refreshed from a good sleep. They may also choose a specific style of venue to create a mood such as austerity, collaboration, conciliation. Or, they may just have need for quick fulfilling closure.

There is a lot to think about and process when big money budgets are in play.

Below are four topics and questions to add to your next sales proposal presentation post mortem:

1. **Their objectives** - Did we do our best job unearthing their true objectives and motives? In my experience, most buyer partners are pretty forthcoming and transparent about what they want, simply because they are trying to foster an environment of trust. Many times, this mindset can lead to collaboration of ideas, which is surely the gold standard in business. Over the years however, there have been a few buyer partners that say one thing and play us to the hilt to get what they truly wanted in a manner that might be construed as feckless and reckless. We always have to ask ourselves, did we really guide them into the bargaining continuum or were we duped?

2. **Tactics they used** - I love the game of tactics in a sales proposal presentation because it is where some of the fine art in deal making is displayed. Tactics are what we see, hear, smell and feel. Can we identify each tactic and catalogue it for the next time with a similar buying partner with an appropriate neutralizer from our side? What verbal expressions did they use? What body language did they present? What did they do to move us off of our script in the heat of the moment? Was there a physical tell when they were getting close to their objectives?

3. **Strategies they used** - The difference between a novice and seasoned buying partner is the strategies they employ. A novice buyer may only have a couple of go to strategies they implement under a wide variety of situations with varied success. Whereas, a seasoned buyer shifts gears with a catalogue of effective strategies like a formula one racecar driver who adapts to the terrain of a high speed track. If you can identify your buyer partner's strategies you have a huge advantage in guiding the other side toward your sales objectives.

4. **Improvements we must make** - The old saying "Fool me once shame on you. Fool me twice shame on me"…applies. In order to become the best sales prospector you can be, you must continually pull even your finest sales efforts apart looking for further improvement. Educate yourself to recognize when a trusted buyer partner is offering you an opening to complete a great innovative

deal. Think more about end-to-end buyer/seller strategies. Understand the importance of your buyer partner's business culture. Think collaboration. Look for the good in buyer partners and conclude smart deals that stand the test of time. Remember, great skill sets take years of practice and refinement. Start your sales proposal presentation post mortem rituals today and begin to make and save more money.

Patrick Tinney

PART 6
SIMPLE NEGOTIATION
STRATEGIES

Patrick Tinney

SEVEN BUYER NEGOTIATION STRATEGIES SALES PROSPECTORS NEED TO KNOW

Perpetual Hunger is a sales prospecting reference book. It is not a sales negotiation book. In doing our best work to prospect for new business we are going to run into customers who not only like our products and services, they need them immediately. Like many savvy buyers these days, they will dangle the carrot of a sale but indicate to us they need something to sweeten the deal before they agree to the deal. Our answer as a seller cannot be, *"Well I am only sales prospecting and selling today. I am not negotiating to get deals done."* Wrong answer. If we see a profitable sale while prospecting and the demands from the buyer's side are not pernicious or outrageous, we definitely want to try to close the deal on the spot. This is especially true if we get the sense this account buyer is looking at us with a longer range view to help them grow their business.

Our goal in this section of *Perpetual Hunger* is to help identify, name, and identify risk for seven negotiation strategies that buyers use. By understanding these strategies, sellers will have a greater opportunity to react quicker to these bargaining strategies. This allows us to weigh our options, neutralize the strategy, or call for a change in strategy to maximize our sales negotiation potential.

At Centroid Training, we love to teach negotiation strategy. These are seven of our favorite easy to understand negotiation strategies. We see these strategies being used on sellers over and over again. Any one of these strategies can be used by buyers singularly or in combination. When used in combination, these negotiation strategies become extra powerful. Sellers stay alert.

1. **Buyer Sells Concept of Yes...Will You Take This Price?**

The "concept of yes ...will you take this price" buyer negotiation strategy is brilliant because the buyer is assuming the role of a seller. The buyer, however, still holds the purse strings on the deal. This strategy is a stinger. The risk for the buyer is very low. The risk for the seller is very high.

The concept of yes is all about compressing the seller's time without the seller being fully aware. In our buyers' market, we experience this strategy as a mainstay for crafty buyers who don't care about fostering close relationships. The seller has to be adroit, with a clear understanding of profit margins and hidden customer value to manage this buyer strategy. The seller also has to be mindful of the full array of pricing they have offered their entire customer base, for fear of a price contagion. The "concept of yes" strategy has no limit on account size. I know of one case where a large advertiser used it on a huge daily newspaper. Therefore, it can be used in large volume negotiations if both buyer and seller are acutely aware of competitive pricing and cost structures.

Tip: If you research your customers well, you can pick off the type of client who will use the "concept of yes". Be sure to have easy access to your client files or pricing channels you offer at all times. If you get squeezed, request a relaxation of time to do the buyer's offer justice. Be creative with your back-up plans. Be careful to limit the duration of a deal you cannot live with over the long haul. Remember, where pricing is concerned, everything leaks.

2.   Buyer Creates a Share & Compare Quote Scheme

"Share & compare" is one of my least favorite buyer strategies. It is a blunt instrument used by aggressive buyers who generally place little value on confidentiality and long-term relationships. The risk for the buyer is low in this environment with the exception of one key area – trust. How can a seller trust a buyer who is using another seller's confidential proposal as a leverage instrument? The risk to the seller is elevated, in that closing a deal with a buyer using this strategy means our seller proposal/deal is now expected to be public knowledge in the foreseeable future. Time compression is reasonably high. The seller will have to make a decision fairly quickly as to whether they want to pursue this business knowing, the buyer could be using the same strategy with several of our competitors simultaneously.

This strategy is a mugs game. And, believe it or not, it has been used by large dollar volume buyers when they feel they need to leverage a deal.

Tip: Visualize working with this customer several years ahead. What does the relationship look like in your mind? How much valuable information can we reasonably pass over to this customer? Do we take this customer our best ideas? Do we treat this relationship as a commoditized strategic sell?

My counsel is to be very "Spartan" with releasing deep data to a customer who is utilizing "share & compare". Know that you are essentially buying the business with this customer. Be prepared for volatility in maintaining this sale as it will always be on the auction block.

3.   Buyer Requests Test Rate Scheme

"Test or pilot rates" really do have a place in Win/Win negotiations. If both sides are sincere in their exploration of a product trial, building a long-term and a trusting relationship using test rates is a great place to start.

Some buyers just use the "test rate" discussion as a window to understand the seller's profitability and lay the groundwork for a discussion around the "test rate" becoming a permanent rate. The thinking from the buyer's side is if you can afford to run a "test rate" this must be close to your profit line. If the buyer starts to understand your profit margins then, the carrot discussion will begin. And the next question will be, "How about a large contract at this test rate?"

This strategy puts great pressure and risk on the seller. The buyer is under some risk, but, always has the option of cancelling a contract if no penalty clauses are spelled out in a signed agreement. Time compression risk can be quite wide with this strategy as the buyer often ends up selling the strategy to the seller.

Tip: As a seller, test or pilot rates really are a great tool in a sales negotiation for a trial. The problem is once introduced to the market; pricing is a hard thing to control. So we have to be very careful with price contagion, especially when dealing with large accounts. The other concern is if the test account really grows dramatically, what does this do to the overall profitability of your seller business? There is nothing worse than having one gigantic account and no profit.

Therefore, when we are heading into a test or pilot program, I recommend putting a time or inventory limit on it. We then blend up the "test rate" with a proposal turning the test rate into normalized pricing consistent with your industry.

4.   Split the Difference Strategy

The "split the difference strategy" is one of the most overused and most misunderstood negotiation strategies ever. There are entire business categories (think Real Estate) that use this negotiation strategy as a foundation. Therefore, as an outsider, if you don't want to play "split the difference" you are in many cases considered rude or uneducated. This last notion is anything but the truth.

The problem with "split the difference" is that it usually benefits the negotiation partner initiating the strategy. Therefore, the risk is laid on the party receiving this negotiation strategy. One more thing, time compression risk can be a big factor. Let me explain. Let's say you see a house for sale at $200,000 and you have a mortgage approval for exactly $180,000. You put an offer of $180,000 thinking the price you are offering is fair after reviewing the house prices in the neighborhood and the condition of the home you are pursuing. The seller wanting to sell at full price says, "I will sell to you if we can split the difference in our valuations". If you accept this offer, the seller has convinced you to raise your bid by $10,000 or approximately 6% over what you thought was fair value for the house. My question is…why would anyone go into a negotiation knowing they will be expected, even cajoled to raise their offer just to appear civil or in good form?   Since we have no opportunity to raise more money, asking for the seller's chattels in the home is pointless.

Tip: If you are negotiating with someone and they say "Come on, let's just split the difference" ask yourself why would this negotiation partner want to do this? Who has the advantage in this scheme?   Smart money says go back and look at your backup plans. If the numbers don't make sense go to your next plan or politely refuse the kind offer.

5.   **Give Small Take Big Strategy**

The "give small take big" strategy is as it sounds. It is similar to a "log rolling strategy" meaning you scratch my back and I'll scratch yours. The idea is that it is reciprocal. The rub in "give small take big" is the reciprocation is not proportionate or even. It is a strategy that has a Win/Lose feel to it depending on how it is executed. Many times it is used to unbalance sellers and occasionally even buyers.

For example, years ago I was asked by a neighbor to help him buy a compact Pontiac car when General Motors decided to discontinue this automobile brand. Dealerships everywhere were selling these cars at a discount. My neighbor had found the car he wanted and he had done some preliminary bargaining. He wanted me in for the last pass of negotiation. From my perspective my neighbor had cut the car price to the bone with the dealership. Knowing this, we asked the dealer for a laundry list of smaller items to close the deal. We suggested three free car detailing appointments, a discount on an extended warranty and a few extra hundred dollars off the price. Owing to the fact that we were asking for some soft cost items to be included in the deal, the sales manager wanted to personally close the deal. Understandably, he didn't want to give us a thing. We were sitting in his office with the sales representative. All of a sudden, one of the sales support staff quietly walked into our negotiation session with a fresh cherry pie and proceeded to tell us because we had test driven the Pontiac we were entitled to the pie. This was all a stratagem. By offering to give us the pie we were expected to acquiesce on something in the deal. I had never seen it done this way but I knew what it was and what was expected of us. I declined the pie explaining to the young sales assistant that we had sugar allergies in our family. This was my way of getting away from the pie. I continued to press for our deal with greater gusto telling the sales manager we had eaten up way too much of his time and that of his staff. I continued by explaining to him that if he let us out of the dealership without selling the car to us as I had recommended, he would never recover the lost time and money. I told the sales manager to sign the deal before we changed our minds, which he did.

Tip: Think about how "give small take big" plays into your world. By analyzing this stratagem you can either employ it in your sales offerings or you can neutralize it as I did. It is not necessarily a malevolent strategy, you just have to think about what you have to offer or take that is meaningful but, not necessarily costly.

6.   **Poor Mouth. "We Have No Money" Strategy**

If I have heard poor mouth once I have heard… "We have no money" as a strategy a hundred times. This strategy is not limited to small businesses truly facing day-to-day survival. Just the opposite is true. Very successful mid-tier and even large corporations use the poor mouth strategy. When larger businesses use this negotiation strategy it is premeditated and it could be cultural.

Be wary of "C Level" officers of businesses who want to probe for information and ask for advice about their problems. When you enquire about budget the violins start to play in the back ground. One CEO who ran a nationally branded company wanted my help and went on to say he ran a rather small company. And, he actually told me he couldn't say for sure that he had any budget. If the CEO does not know about his budget we have a problem.

In larger corporations, poor mouth "we have no money" is used citing limited departmental budgets and argues any funds that they do have must be stretched until their year-end.

Tip: When exposed to the poor mouth strategy let your profitability and cost modeling be your guide. Don't get drawn in by all of the false theatrics. Remember…when we negotiate in good faith, we must be allowed to be profitable. Otherwise, we are being used.

Patrick Tinney

7.   **The "Growing List" Strategy-** We have to pay very close attention to professional buyers who chip away at our profitability in a sales negotiation by insidiously adding pieces into a deal of which they have no intention of paying. In the "growing list" strategy buyers gently nudge us to comply with requests for an upgrade here and a freebie there until the deal starts to feel a little lopsided.

These add on requests can happen at the front of a deal or the back of a deal. I had one customer who would meet with me and pretend to be moving toward a deal. He would start to get into the details of the deal until important information was shared from our side that could well be considered billable information. He would pause for a moment and say something to the effect of "Thank you for sharing but, don't bill me for that". He was using his leverage at the front end of the deal to extract extra value before we could even get a real idea how big the budget was. He was very adroit with this "growing list" strategy. Other buyers simply try to pressure us at the end of a deal while signing the deal. They continue the conversation with "I know this means nothing to you but could you please tuck in a couple of XY & Z's to as a show of good faith on your side?" By doing this the buyer places us in an uncomfortable position. We either accept this "growing list" of items at no cost in his/her version of good faith or it forces us to push back. This makes us look like a nickel squeezing seller partner.

Tip: Make sure you keep a running total on the true value and cost of any "growing list" items added into a deal without expected payment. Make the customer aware of the real value of these items. If the items are too costly, I recommend asking for something from the customer to justify this increased cost. In other words, see if you can get them to expand the pie a bit. You don't have to win the entire argument with this approach. You just want to make sure the customer knows you are looking for a collaborative business partner. One who realizes you as a seller must be profitable. If the customer listens to you with some sense of empathy and adds a little more to their side of the deal, you know you have a great relationship in the making. If the customer shrugs you off as if their behavior is normal and should be accepted, keep a really close eye on your costs. I recommend you limit your exposure to customers who treat you in this manner.

STRATEGY SUMMARY

The seven buyer negotiation strategies I have shared with you are being used by your customers on an hourly and daily basis. Therefore, it is in your best interest to sharpen your sales negotiation game. You must learn to identify these strategies early in negotiations. Learn how to neutralize them or reroute them into a less competitive and more collaborative based channel. What makes all of these strategies even more effective and compelling is that buyers are using these strategies by phone, e-mail, and Skype. This means that as a seller, you are losing more and more face-time with your customers. This means you do not have the ability to read your negotiation partner's face and body movements, so critical to understanding how stressed or how serious they really are. It says to me, we must raise our sales negotiation game even if we are sales prospecting and not expecting to close a deal this way. We must do our best to pull game theory based agreements toward more amicably based negotiations where both parties are permitted to be profitable. We want strong, smart, relationship based deals that stand the test of time.

Patrick Tinney

FINAL THOUGHTS

Sales prospecting is eternally and constructively tied to consultative selling and sales negotiation. Therefore, we must always be very mindful of the power and strength of long-term trusting businesses relationships. Armor-piercing questions in various forms must not be seen as anything other than a positive risk tool.

Our personal brand is nothing more than our personal set of perfectly repeatable promises at work. It's how we sell ideas. It's how we prepare show stopping proposals. It's how we conduct and manage all aspects of selling and presenting long-term value to great new customers.

After reading *Perpetual Hunger,* I hope you will clearly see how sales prospecting is a great hunting expedition comprised of philosophy, theory, soft skills and art. Sales prospecting, at the boardroom table, on the phone and in e-mail is a canvas of unfettered creativity. It is a rolodex of plans and back-up plans that lead us into profitable, long-term business relationships.

Preparation and practice cannot be understated. To be a truly great sales prospector, you must be prepared to put in the work to make it happen. There will be great sales prospecting days and there will be days that will leave us wanting. This is normal. Remember nothing in life is free. Great prospectors try, learn and express positive risk as a way of life. This might sound a little too philosophical, but, I can assure you the great sales prospectors are always developing templates. They develop systems to speed up the sales prospecting process. The great sales prospectors are fearless. They know that a modicum of failure is just a test to help them reset their coordinates, retool and get running straight toward epic wealth and wonderful new customers. Our knowledge of strategy and our ability to shift strategy in the blink of an eye makes us a powerful force.

Remember, the world of sales prospecting is an ever changing environment based on competition, product development and technology. We must continue to add new tools to our sales prospecting repertoire. Read, practice, and implement bravely.

Be creative. Offer great value. Make friends. Be true to yourself.

Last thought….think, act and be in a constant state of *"Perpetual Hunger"*.

ACKNOWLEDGEMENTS

I cannot imagine writing a book in total isolation.

This important list of people helped, pushed, pulled, cajoled, and cheered me on as I saw the light in *Perpetual Hunger: Sales Prospecting Lessons & Strategy.*

Please accept my gratitude:

Paul Brown	Ed "Skip" McLaughlin
Steve Cosic	Graeme Ross
Randy Craig	Stan Shortt
Margaret Hall	Ken Smith
Bob Hollings	Barbara Tinney
Chris Kata	Connie Tinney
David Kingsmill	Sean Tinney
Mary Jo Krump	David Titcombe
Steve Macfarlane	…..to mention a few.

Also a special thank you to Glenn Marshall and The Greening Marketing Team www.greeningmarketing.ca for their expert knowledge on publishing and cover design. Smart people executing on what they do best.

Patrick Tinney

REFERENCES

Although I did not directly quote any other published book sources, I did refer to and take inspiration from the following fine authors on creativity, consultative selling, strategy & negotiation.

Edward de Bono. Six Thinking Hats 1985, 1999, 2000

Joe Girard. How to Sell Anything to Anybody 1978

214

INDEX

Build effective skills that matter through

WORKSHOPS

KEYNOTES

BUSINESS & PITCH COACHING

CONSULTATIONS

Author, Patrick Tinney is an experienced sales professional who shares his real life, real deal experiences with audiences across all business categories. Patrick lives and practices the principles of sales prospecting and sales negotiation addressed in his writings. Business leaders count on Patrick's unwavering commitment to their success.

Centroid Training & Marketing

Helping business make and save money.

Bus: (705) 657-2518 Mobile: 416-617-3271

E-mail: patrick@centroidmarketing.com

www.centroidmarketing.com

NOTES

NOTES

NOTES

NOTES

CPSIA information can be obtained
at www.ICGtesting.com
Printed in the USA
BVHW01s1355061217
502112BV00010B/366/P